D0587559

20 OCT 2012 18 NOV 2011

Please return or renew this
item by the last date shown.
Books may also be
renewed by phone or internet

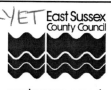

RYET East Sussex
County Council

eastsussex.gov.uk

**East Sussex Library and information Services
eastsussex.gov.uk/libraries**

My Father's Keeper

SHE HAD TO PROTECT HIM. HE MADE HER PROMISE.
SHE WAS HIS 10-YEAR-OLD DAUGHTER.

JULIE GREGORY

HarperElement
An Imprint of HarperCollins*Publishers*
77–85 Fulham Palace Road,
Hammersmith, London W6 8JB

www.harpercollins.co.uk

and *HarperElement* are trademarks
of HarperCollins*Publishers* Ltd

First published by HarperCollins*Publishers* 2008
This edition 2009

2

A catalogue record for this book
is available from the British Library

ISBN 978-0-00-726880-1

Printed and bound in Great Britain by
Clays Ltd, St Ives plc

The Children of Happiness

They are to be cherished and protected,
Even at the risk of your life.
They know sadness but will overcome it.
They know alienation
For they see past and through this reality.
They will *Endure* where others cannot.
They will *Survive* where others cannot.
They know love even when it is not shown to them.
They spend their lives trying to communicate the
love they know.

Chapter One

I was born on the day of Liberace, May 16th to be exact, The Day of Outrageous Flair. In the *Big Blue Birthday* book, Outrageous Flair is appropriately illustrated by a snapshot of Liberace himself soaking in a marbled bath as bottomless as deep dish apple pie, the round of the tub one white solid bubble. The showman and pianist was in his golden age, as plump and gaudy as Elvis in those final days of Vegas. Marinating in bubbles, his stout fingers spread by thick, jewelled rings, he flashes that champagne smile, beaming squarely at the camera from between two gilded swan neck faucets.

At the time that picture was snapped, I was a stick figure tweeny living in a trailer out in southern Ohio, on the back woods edge of a dead end country road that held as many secrets as it lacked street lights. My tub was shallow and rectangular and moulded of the same gold plastic as the trailer's doorknobs. The bent-necked swans my mother had gold leafed were also plastic and hung slightly ajar on the bathroom's wood panelling. The constant burning of bacon in the kitchen had infused our trailer's hermetically sealed air with a sort of permanent tack that coated the curved backs of the swans and caught whatever floated through the bathroom, making a sort of three-dimensional dust. It gave the swans a hairy appearance – not unlike the very chest of Liberace himself.

My father's baby blue polyester suit hung in the closet and his white Vegas-style loafers lounged beneath, their tight backs ready to snap around his heels and rub blisters. I can still see him wince as he hobbled along after only an hour in them. My mother's cubic zirconia rings sat in an Avon dish on the back of the toilet, next to the Stick Up.

There was no cameraman and certainly no smiling.

As a young girl, I was taller than I was wide. Long, cool and lanky, I took my strides with the measured gait of an Arabian filly. It wasn't something I tried for, it just happened. And when I walked the halls as a new Jr. High student, the senior boys called me highwater for the long legs that seemed destined to greatness. I should have been a ballerina, or a model, or at least a prima donna. But sometimes the stork drops you in the wrong place.

Because for all the feel and longing inside me to be a noble child of royal descent, even of the Liberace kind, there was no way around the blaring, honking reality of my daily life: I was shackled to a family of losers.

There was my dad with his *Mork from Ork* suspenders worn long after it was cool and his battery-operated bull horn that he snuck into football games. And Mom with her outdated fringed western gear making me couple skate with her to Peaches and Herb's "*Reunited*" at the Make-A-Date Roller Skating Rink in Amanda, Ohio.

Thank God it was the next town over.

And I guess it wouldn't have been so bad if my dad wasn't ooga-ing his horn every time a junior in tight Jordache jeans walked in front of the bleachers. And the girls, with their sixth sense, would slow in their tracks for instinctual preening, pulling Goody combs from back pockets to feather long layers back along the sides of their heads, all the while tilting gently parted mouths in just such a way as to showcase their teeth. Then they'd dart glances up into the bleachers trying to catch the eye of their suitor.

I could have died.

And so could they when they spotted my dad; large, hairy, menacing, looking a cross between Jerry Garcia and Charles Manson in rainbow suspenders, wiggling his fat fingers, "Yoooo-hoooo," at them like he would to a baby. They bolted and my dad would raise his megaphone and blitz the button for the Dukes of Hazzard's car horn, blaring the confederate tune into the crisp fall night, adding his own *"Charge!"* at the end and springing to his feet. I wedged my body down into the foot bleachers and unfolded my turtleneck in triplicate up over my nose, hoping this alone would shield my identity.

And when I wasn't saddled with him on game Fridays, I was stuck with Mom on the Saturdays, dragging me out under the swooning lights of the rink just so she wouldn't have to couple skate alone. She was upping her chances to catch a wink from the married owner by getting out on the floor when it was least populated.

I held her sweaty hand and we coasted with locked knees around pitted wooden corners, while dancing polka dot lights spun me dizzy on the dark floor.

Reunited And It Feeels So Goood.

Trust me. No kid wants their 40-year-old mother asking them if her butt looks okay in the skating rink bathroom.

* * *

I was desperate. Desperate to get out of the hollow where I lived with the big trucks with gun racks in the back and bumper stickers that read *"Boobs, Booze, and Country Music"*, where at least one hand-lettered yard sign on the way to town scolded with a twang:

> *This is God's Country*
> *Don' drive through it like Hell*

I wanted far away from the kids my dad cornered at the football game's concession stand, demanding they tell him how cool he was – the same ones that went on to pelt the back of my head with crabapples the rest of the year on the school bus. Like it or not, by the very virtue of association, I was a loser too; as long as I was under my father's roof, every fledgling step in the teenage social hierarchy was eclipsed by a trademark faux pas of my father – a public squelch, raucous belch or exaggerated, lingering crotch adjustment.

The fall of eighth grade saw me herded into choir with the rest of the class, and despite complaining along with the other kids over the injustice and uncoolness of it all, I was secretly thrilled to be looped into the pomp and circumstance of school perform-ance, a world I'd never have gained entry to if it was not mandatory for the class. My parents, in all their

5

trailer-minded glory, placed zero importance on the intellectual advancement of anything as meaningless as music or art. School was seen as a sort of extended daycare to keep me out of the house until I got off the bus and could be handed a list of chores that wouldn't cease until bedtime. To say that school – and all the bells and whistles of extracurricular activities – meant nothing to them was an understatement.

Choir was the first indulgence of any kind I'd had, the music room a luxurious epicentre of civilized culture that offset the glare of my trailer tarnish.

Our first performance of the year was marked by flat grey skies pregnant with the fall of winter's virgin snow. The sky hung small and low over the miles of brittle brown corn fields that surrounded Mcdowell middle school but it wasn't the gloom of winter that knitted my forehead as my father drove us there.

"Dad?"

"Yeah, honey?"

"Promise you won't embarrass me?"

"Embarrass you?" he snorted. "What, you don't think your old man's cool? I know what cool is. I'm so cool I had tattoos on my diapers."

"Just promise," I pleaded as I stared out of the window, watching the bitter wind kick corn husks up into swirling funnel clouds.

We stood at the mouth of the auditorium, my father and I, his sideburns thick as mutton chops and with that trademark chipmunk smile, the top teeth forced over the bottom giving his grin, however manly he may be, a forever permanence of being twelve. He wore polyester and I wore corduroy and putty-coloured panty hose, a fresh snag running up my leg. In our first formal event together, my father pretended to wait for someone, craning his neck up and over the families that bustled around us and took their seats in the auditorium once they embraced each other. So confident of his cool in the car, he had started to sweat. A few beads of perspiration popped up on his forehead; one let loose and trickled down into his sideburn like a checker dropped from his hairline.

I knew I would have to stay. Who knows what might happen if I left his side?

The wind instruments began their warm up. My choir teacher swept past on her way to the stage and stopped to collect me, placing her delicate conductor's hand softly on my back. I can still feel the exact outline of it singed on my back.

My father thrust his arm out to her, erupting in a boyish grin and my choir teacher, never the wiser, stretched her long tapered fingers to his, slipping a dainty palm into his calloused one.

I caught the twinkle in his eye but it was too late.

In the split second it takes for the little squeeze that accompanies a handshake, my father cocked his left leg and farted in the empty hall.

Dad roared maniacally. My choir teacher recoiled her hand in horror as my father held it steadfast. And I, the delicate child, stood alone between them. This was life with my dad.

As humiliating as it was to be out in public with my father, I needed him too. He pointed out kids who made fun of me and without him, I felt exposed and uncertain of how to interpret the world around me. Luckily, our public outings were rare. My father wanted little more than to be parked in his La-Z-Boy recliner in the small cavern of our trailer's living room, cocooned by the soft glow of six to eight hours of television a night. Dad was perfectly content to recline in a flat, predictable world, experienced in manageable half-hour increments, with nothing more complex than a riveting episode of *Sanford and Son*.

There was me, Danny, my little brother, Mom and Dad, all living in a mobile home that started out no bigger than the trailer of a semi truck. But each of us was living in our own fantasy.

At night I lay in bed burning; burning in a vision of running away. I would get on *The Price Is Right*, "*Julie Gregory, C'mon down! You're the next contestant on the*

Price Is Right," I would spring five perfect back flips down the aisle – *boom* – straight onto contestant's row. I'd lean into the mike and know the actual retail price of the His-n-Hers matching hi-ball glasses, the numbers rolling out my mouth like Pentecostal tongue. I'd play the Mountain Climber game with the grace and ease of a cut-throat watcher. And the way I span the wheel, you'd think I had one set up at home in the wood-panelled basement.

After winning both prizes in the Showcase Show-down, my carefully studied bid falling within buckshot of a hundred dollars of my own well-chosen showcase, I'd step out from behind my podium; pry the mike from Bob's cold, tan fingers and croon, *"This is Julie Gregory for Bob Barker, reminding you to help control the pet population! Have your pet spayed or neutered!"*

Bob would fall silent, pursing that thin smile as he clamoured for control. But I could tell he was impressed.

Showgirls would fan out around me to fill in for the lack of family rushing the stage and I'd whisper that I'd be donating at least one of the cars to the Humane Society. One showgirl would cup her hand to Bob's ear and he, in turn, would tell the audience. The crowd went wild.

"Who is this amazing teenage girl?" hissed down the aisles like brushfire.

I lay in bed at night, the vision searing behind my eyes; my fingers clasped upon my soft-breathing belly, eyes wide open, boring into the dark.

And while I was running away to Burbank, California, Mom was living in a closet of gold lamé tracksuits, each holding in its folds the golden promise of an imaginary cruise drifting on the horizon of a fading sunset. The ensembles jammed to swelling on her closet rod, each with its respective price tag dangling anxiously in case the cheque bounced.

And while Mom spent her nights trying on outfits for the ritzy vacation that never came, my little brother Danny lived in a fortress constructed of hundreds and hundreds of Matchbox cars, to which he was ruler of their domain, and future race car driver of all. For those that were his favourites, he had a special carry bag in which he stacked them double decker and carried like an attaché case at all times. In the space between our fantasy bubbles, the air of the trailer was charged electric, ready to crack with velocity the minute one of these worlds tilted toward reality. But the truth was that even as my father lay dormant in a homogenized state, rich in his lazy life, even as he rooted at football games in his ridiculous suspenders and insisted he was the King of Cool, in the front pocket of his trousers sat a spring-loaded gun. It stayed put in my father's pocket twenty-four hours a day.

He didn't even take it out at night, just dropped his pants and stepped out of two perfect trouser tunnels – leaving his .25 like a sleeping watchdog on the floor by the bedside.

And if he couldn't get to it, there was always the gun kept beneath his pillow and the other two tucked under my mother's wigs in the bathroom cupboard. Failing those, three sat atop the refrigerator – one at the front, one in the middle closest to the stove and the third at the very back in case the one or both of the other two were stolen.

And those were just the guns inside.

Hidden beneath a stack of Taco Bell napkins in the glove compartment of the car was yet another – with an extra gun tucked under the springs of the driver's seat, just in case.

But the one constant was my father's .25. It was always with him, in the La-Z-Boy, at church and even as the eighth grade choir warbled through *Englasis On High*. And each day, without really knowing it, I was holding my breath, right up to my fifteenth birthday when my father took his gun to the rooftop of the Sherex Chemical Company to jump.

By then, my father had come to spook easy. And it was my job to ease him out of it. In this way, I was his watchdog too. Tension strung in trap wires around him and anything could pluck the strings: a door slammed by the breeze, the backfire of a muffler, a hunter's random gunshot that pierced the silence of our woods and my father's corresponding jolt, duck, a violent swing of his head, the injection of panic into the air from his electrified body sending a ripple effect through me. When he jumped, I jumped. So having Dad in the La-Z-Boy meant a break from the worry. My father was like his gun; the safety latch might be on, but it could go off anytime.

It wasn't until I had a life of my own, free from my own jolts and ducks and wide eyes that swung around wildly, that I could lay claim to the feeling, to understand that what lay just under the surface of my father's happy-go-lucky appearance, and resonated out into our family through the conduit of myself, was something so big, so incomprehensible that it could never be touched or opened by any words or healed by the passage of time. And to a kid, that was far larger than anything spoken at all.

There was so much craziness that went down back then, so much Technicolor madness that defied anyone in the Tri-County area from ever believing it, that I'm surprised we even made it out as a family. And by family I don't just mean the initial clan of us, the four of us who were at best odd-shaped puzzle pieces from entirely different boxes, but the extended cache of strangers that were folded into our drama along the way. Because honestly, without the punctuation of their presence and the adrenaline that swirled around it, I don't think I could have stood another day with the suspenders or the bullhorn, the skates or the fringed western wear without grabbing at least one of the guns off the top of the fridge and blowing my brains out.

Chapter Two

Even though my father came of age in the Sixties, he was cut of a different cloth than the era. My dad never went to Woodstock. He didn't protest the war. He did not wear leather vests or fringy things. Never in his life did he don sandals or moccasins, smoke pot or down a fifth of whiskey. And I don't think my dad even knew what the term "tie-dye" meant. He was a lanky sprout of a kid with Alfred E. Newman ears that sprung out from the side of his head and a smirk that turned him into a west side slurpee the second he flashed it.

He dropped out of school at the age of seventeen to register for Vietnam because he thought the uniform would get him girls. And when the officer that brought him on pitched an extra week of leave for every friend he signed up with him, he volunteered the names of his three best buddies, walked out of the recruiter's office and promptly blew off boot camp to take his three promised weeks off. He was AWOL before he even began.

My own mother had scarcely made it through the ninth grade when she was married off by her mother, my Grandma Madge, to a carny – what those who worked in the carnivals called themselves – in his fifties named Smokey. At the same time Dad was doing his two months overseas, Mom was travelling with the Grand Ole Opry, trick riding horses and being one half of a side-winding whip act, all in fringed leather. The original white showman's jacket she wore before I was born hung in my trailer closet as a teenager, radiating the smell of decaying leather and mothballs.

Mom and father, both from the west side of Columbus, existed thousands of miles apart until the trajectory of their lives careened them into one another with a violent crash. Within the span of a few months, my dad was flown back to the States from Vietnam and checked into his first government-issue psychiatric ward and Mom was a widow after walking in to find a cold, stiff Smokey propped up in bed. It was only later I'd hear the whispers that she'd been questioned about his death.

16

When my dad came out of the mental hospital at age 20, he took the first job he could get at the gas station at Grant and Sullivan. Mom pulled in and less than a month shy of Smokey being cold in the ground had a real boyfriend lined up. Their first official date was on Valentine's Day; they married in March. Six months later a baby was on the way. That baby was me.

I guess looking back there were signs all along, ominous forewarnings that we would all end piled up at the bottom of that dead-end dirt road desperate and feral as a trapped cat. And the lynchpin of them all orbited around my father and the first singular memory I have of him just shy of turning four.

I remember we lived on Cedarleaf Road in Ohio.

I remember the picnic table in the backyard was a giant wooden spool for electrical wire which Dad had rolled home from the base where he worked.

I remember getting parked on top of the refrigerator when *Planet of the Apes* came on, my father's reason being I'd sit still straight through to the commercials if I was afraid of tipping off.

And I remember looking out the living room window from behind heavy mustard-coloured curtains to see my father on his hands and knees in the gravel drive.

He had come home early after being fired.

He pushed a jack under the sedan, hiked his pants up by the loops and plastered a shock of greasy hair across his forehead. I watched his skinny arm pump as the car began to rise.

When it was high enough to teeter, he got down in the gravel and shimmied up flat under the car, his fingers inching out to grasp the rusty frame. In slow motion, he began to rock; back and forth, back and forth, until his body slid out from under the chaises with each hoist of his arms; like a low, heavy chin-up.

I was standing at the storm door by now, watching through the glass when Mom sauntered up behind me. Her arms grazed my hair as they folded into lock-down over her chest, the heat of bristle rolling off her. And it was then that I first felt the gulf between the rest of the world and my father, a chasm so dark and bottomless that even then I sensed it could swallow him whole.

But in that moment I also knew that I would reach across and save him. I would be his bridge back. And in reaching for my father, I would not let him fall.

The car swayed lightly, his face wedged under the tyre and with every rock my body winched forward, until it pressed solid against the pane wet with cold. I touched my fingertips to the glass and bore my eyes steady into the front end of the car. I would not let it fall.

"Jesus," Mom hissed, "He can't even do that right."
I stared harder, willing the car to stay.
On my father rocked.
And it was only me that stood between them.

That's where my father remains forever etched in my being: just out of reach, on the other side of the glass. From that day forward, carved in my heart was a hole which no other love but his could fill. With a fragile liability that led him out to the drive to wedge himself under the car and a three-year-old omnipotent enough to feel she alone could save him, we were crippled from the start. But this was the template from which my love was stamped and I could no sooner change it than a duckling could undo its imprinting at birth.

Like the Quakers, the Gregory family lineage had always managed to linger slightly on the brink of extinction. My mother's dad put a gun in his mouth when she was still a girl, my dad's mother died young of a stroke, his own father only hovered above death, living in a perpetual alcoholic stupor behind cases of Bud Light stacked to the ceiling to keep out the light of day. And, with the eventual death of the last withered-up great-grandparent, the first portrait of our remaining family clan is snapped.

It is a blustery, winter afternoon in Columbus, Ohio, on a piss-grey day, lined up next to a cement wall cascading the carcass of a bush that used to be alive in the months of green.

There is something to be said for the fashion of the Seventies; something haunting, almost surreal in what people actually wore out into the world. In this photo, it's all of us and we amount to only five – six if you count the dog my grandmother's holding.

There's Lee, my mother's mentally slow brother, standing on the one end, pelvis tilted forward, shoulders slack, arms stiff at his sides. Grandma Madge, my mother's mother, is next to him, oozing eternal Christian goodness out her every pore. She has a pulsating cluster of fabric orchids fingering out over her lapel and there is something almost sinister to them, like an accessory The Joker might wear. Mom is next to Grandma Madge in a long blond and black peppered wig that kind of makes her look like an early cone head, from where the seam sewn at the top points into a little ^ that runs down her scalp. She wears a purple mini with one panty-hosed knee cocked like a model's.

Then there's Dad on the end. Standing cockeyed, throwing the camera his pissed-off, I-could-just-kill-you glare, having hoisted me up to his chest with one mighty palm and pointing his leg out away from the rest of us, like he was about to get off the exit ramp of this family any minute now. His clip-on tie hangs limp and is tucked into a wrinkled suit coat with a buckling waist button, too small to span his protruding belly, even though his pant legs hang ghostly empty.

As Dad points away from the other three, looking disgusted, Lee, on the other end, bears down into the heels of his shoes, looking constipated. I sit on the shelf of my father's arm and beam brightness in my funeral dress, lacy bonnet and white ribbed leggings. And it is after this funeral that we do what most thinning, dysfunctional families do: move cross country to be closer to one another.

I have no other photo of my father and me until the age of nine and by then my brother Danny will have joined us, amping our total extended family count up to six. But until then, there are seven delicious years of just me and my dad.

It is 1973 in Phoenix, Arizona, and I am four years old. I have a Fisher-Price Castle and Weebles "wobble but they don't fall down". The plastic horses are thick and smooth and their legs move at the joints, and the castle has a dungeon where the innocent await rescue. They just don't make toys like that anymore.

On the first day after our arrival, my father and I are dropped off in a public park while our mother drives around to scout for a place to live. Six years his senior, her 31 to his green 25 entitled her to make every choice that affected us, from where we lived to when we moved. Dad lounged in the lush grass, not a care in the world and peeled off a mound of marshmallow snow-ball from its wrapper to hand over to me. It was the most delicious thing I had eaten in all of my four years and we lazed in the grass, licking coconut marshmal-low off our fingers; every moment stolen with my father one of pure contentment knowing he was safe with me.

In our rented crackerjack house, my days are spent parked in front of the television set in a sunken den of the Seventies, covered in wall-to-wall wine-coloured shag. Dad looks for work and Mom slumps at the dinette in the kitchen, smoking cigarettes and push-ing the cuticles back on her nails.

"Look, Julie, you're father's an ass, alright?" she'd startle when I'd catch her talking to herself. "So what if he does find work?" She blew smoke over my head from one of the emergency fags she kept stashed in the silverware drawer, "He couldn't keep a job if his ass was on fire."

It was a bad disposition and sheer idiocy, Mom insisted, that caused Dad to get fired. And the more he shied from her verbal assaults, the more I spread my wings to shelter him. If I could temper his mood and happiness, it seemed a small price to pay to have my father by my side. The details were never quite clear but, if there is one thing I can attest to with consistency about my father, it is that whatever misfortune happened along the way, it was never, ever his fault. Bound to see him through his own eyes, it would take me twenty odd years to trace the wreckage back to its source.

My father has the deepest dimples: craters carved into the sides of his face that when activated, all joy sprang forth and radiated outward. My father might not smile for the camera, but he lights up when he sees me. He bounds through the door at the end of the day and scoops me up and I wrap my arms around his neck, squeezing tight. He flips me upside down and swings me by my ankles, my long blond hair tumbling down. He draws my back to his chest with one arm, with me still upside down and pretends to stumble like a blind man into the living room, jutting his other hand out to feel the way. I giggle wildly as he steadies a faux fall down to the carpet, digging his fingers into my armpits until I laugh so hard I nearly wet my pants.

"Ah, baby, I love you."

"I love you too, Daddy," I say breathless.

He kisses my forehead. I fold his arms around me and brush the soft warm of his palms down over my eyes. I love these moments with my father more than anything.

"Sit on my feet so I can do my sit-ups, baby."

My father calls me baby, a dizzying siren song to my ears. He lay down on his back, bends his knees. I plunk upon my father's toes, leveraging my hands on his ankles. He curls into a sit-up and raises his feet too, lifting me like a see-saw.

"Daddddddd!" I cling to his shins for balance while he tries to buck me off.

"C'mon Baby," he says, as he shakes me from his legs like a lemon from the tree, "You got to hold daddy's feet down!"

I am all gums and teeth with laughter. I bear my weight on the tops of his feet, he crosses his arms on his chest and groans his first sit-up. One, two, three … four … fivvvve … sixsss … he falls back to the floor, winded.

"Six is enough for today, baby." He wheezes and curses under his breath, "Fuckin' Agent Orange."

My mother slices through the corner of the living room, carrying stacks of sorted laundry. My father lies on the carpet, clutching his chest – still burning from a faraway place called 'Nam.

"Dan, would you brush your daughter's hair? God, it's a rat's nest. The brush is in my purse."

My father blinks his Little Orphan Annie eyes and crawls over to dig through her bag. I stand between his folded knees and he brushes me from the top, pulling the bristles through my long, fine hair until it snaps in tiny knots at the end. I yelp.

"Jesus Dan, brush her from the bottom, not the top you idiot." She grabs the brush from my father and pulls it hard through my hair, "Like this," then slaps the handle back in his hand.

And my father blinks empty, starts over, follows orders, tries to please.

I didn't meet another child until I was five years old and Mom finally ventured out of the house to find the neighbours. Marty is the Mexican boy from next door who is a year younger and bangs on our door at the crack of dawn; Jill is the girl across the street who is a year older and cheats openly at Hungry Hippos.

At my house we drape the blankets from the bed over the dining room table to make a fort beneath. Mom sits in the kitchen, filing her nails.

And that's when Marty takes me into the bedroom and Jill makes me lay on my bedspread face down.

"We're going to play doctor now," she says in her bossy voice, "I'm the nurse and you need a shot." She pulls my shorts down and my *Tuesday* underwear to the tops of my legs and Marty makes his papery finger-nails into a C and pinches them closed on the skin of my bottom.

25

A dizzying electric current shoots down my legs and out the top of my head from the single vortex of one pinch. I lay there breathing into the pillow.

"That's it." Jill play-slaps my butt. "You were a good patient."

In afternoons of deathly quiet, Mom draws the curtains to shut out the blazing Arizona sun and I play the game of Matching Pairs. I slap the cards down on the carpet and I'm good. I only have to turn them over a couple times before I remember where the exact match is. Apple to apple, orange to orange, flower to flower, I stack the matched sets one on top of the other until everything is paired. Then I shuffle them fancy like I see Mom do at solitaire and do it all over again.

An endless stream of unemployed days comes to an end and my father rushes in to grab me, cupping his big hands over my face and leading me out the door into the drive.

"Lookie, baby, lookie what Daddy got! I saw it and said 'I have got to get that for my baby.'"

In the drive sits a tiny car, a 1972 Datsun painted green, the precise colour of split pea soup.

My father has landed a job as a plumber at the local Air Force base – a position he is almost guaranteed never to lose. Military bases are full of sinks and toilets and drains. In his excitement on the way home, he saw the car and bought it with the money we had left.

"It looks like a peanut, Daddy."

Dad claps his hands, "That's it! That's what we'll call it, my baby's peanut mobile."

My mother simmers at the door as Dad snaps me into the bucket seat. We take off around the block, my hand clinging to the armrest, my head barely high enough to see out the window. My father smiles down to me and I scrunch my shoulders and smile back. The car zips down the road like a Tylenol capsule on wheels, bounding inches above the pavement; racing along with all the punch of a rip cord toy car.

I'm curled in my father's lap for Saturday morning cartoons when he gives me the signal to follow. He silently trips the latch on the screen and pushes me out the door.

"Sandy," he leans back over the threshold, "Me and Julie's going out in the peanut mobile."

I can hear her *No!* from the kitchen but we're already gone; my father exaggerating a tiptoe in fast motion across the pavement while I plaster my hand over my mouth to keep from giggling out loud. He squeals out the drive.

"Just like the Keystone Cops!" he shouts.

"Yeah!"

There is a feeling of exhilaration to be with my father, to escape from the house and have it be just us. Forever bonded; me and my dad. We don't even have to talk. We drive out of our middle class suburb and through tidy neighborhood streets with Monopoly houses and green lawns, the jitter of sprinklers rapid firing across wet grass. We drive into foreign streets with dirt lots by the buildings, where neon signs light Martini glasses with a bikini-clad girl dipping over the side in an illusion of bright lights. Tall, lithe dogs shoot across the road without looking; their big, boney skulls slung low on the prowl.

Dad is taking me for the first time to his favourite Chinese restaurant.

The parking lot is empty. He opens the front door and a brilliant slice of light cuts into the dark. The carpet is sticky under the soles of my white sandals. There are no other people and not even tables set. He lifts me to the black high back of a barstool that is one in a row lining a long bar.

"Be right back, Daddy's gotta go potty."

My father slips through a set of swinging red shutters that hinge in a naked doorway at the end of the bar. Hushed whispers float from behind the shutters and I see a pair of woman's legs rise from sitting under the frame. Minutes tick by with only the occasional rustle – the clamour of a falling pan, a single thud

28

against a wall, another wave of frenzied whispers –
that lets me know my father is still back there.

A long mirror runs behind the bar. If I kneel on the
stool, my head crests into reflection and my face
emerges in the dim light. Over the door behind me, I
can see in the mirror a red exit marquee, and to the left
a barely lit bathroom sign emitting the low sick buzz
of electricity.

The bell on the door tinkles, a wedge of light slashes
across the carpet.

Where is my dad?

A man stands just inside the door, adjusting to the
dark.

I watch him in the glass, frozen in place.

He squints his eyes and slowly makes out my face
in the mirror. He bolts to the men's room just as my
father swings the red lacquered doors open.

"Daddy!"

A woman follows, dressed in pink satin.

"Hi, Baby. Can you say, Sawatdee Cup? That
means 'Hello, how are you' in Taiwanese."

The girl smiles and slips behind the bar. Her long
black hair runs cool down her back. My dad gives the
doorknob of my knee a honk honk. He orders us
wonton soup and egg rolls with duck sauce.

Behind the bar, our waitress turns to give us our
drinks. I glare at her.

She smiles.

My father winks.

He is jovial, relaxed, blowing on my wonton soup to cool it, giving me feathery tickles under my chin, making up for leaving his baby in a way only a dad can do. And in the flicker of a moment, the space between us closes and it's once again a Saturday with just me and my dad.

That first summer in Phoenix was so hot you couldn't touch your bare feet to the sidewalk past morning light. Our reasons for moving close to Grandma Madge were fading as Mom bickered with her over everything from whether a red bell pepper was called a "mango" to the boxes of floor-length dresses Grandma Madge kept in a big box marked "Church Bizarre". She dragged them out from the spare bedroom and held them up against me. Floor-length frocks made of heavy velvet and scratchy gold lamé; high collars, dowdy sleeves, zippered backs. These were not the dresses on their way to the church bazaar, they were in fact rejects coming from it.

"Thanks Madge, that's great, why don't you just keep them for Julie until she's big enough?"

"What a good idea, how old do you think she'll need to be?"

"Twenty, Madge. Twenty."

And Grandma Madge counts on her fingers, pondering aloud where she will store them for fifteen years.

In the beginning my grandmother would take me for day trips to fish at the lake but every car ride home ended in a fender bender with her behind the wheel. Privileges were reeled in to the local Encino Park where she could pedal me around the lake in the Swan boats. But even then Grandma Madge never missed a chance for ministry on the fly and she'd sweep right past the water in one of her to-the-ankle long-sleeved dresses looking for a gang of homeless youths, me in tow.

When she spotted a kid high as a kite with a bloody nose, she made a bee-line for him. The kid looked around, trapped. With nothing else to lose, he closed his eyes as Grandma Madge fished a Bible from her purse. Caught in the rapture of spirit, she began to weep; one woman in prayer, her bony hand bound to the wrist of the bleeding boy. And the Swan boats floated by as the kid sneezed and splattered blood on me from his broken nose while Grandma Madge tried to convert him to Christianity. It was soon decided that only my mother's presence could assure my safety.

I have only one photo from these rare outings with Mom as chaperone. The three of us are leaving the mall, my grandmother with a purse as big as a bowling ball bag looped over the crook of her arm. We have walked out into the parking lot's bright sun and Mom has whacked me on the head with her fist. As I stand heaving in a pastel jumper with knobbly knees and long blond hair, she roots through her purse for the camera and passes it to Grandma Madge. And there we are, a snapshot captured in time, me wiping away a tear and my mother's arm around my shoulder, veneered smile sealed upon her face.

To her credit, I always remember Mom having a soft spot for animals and back then she'd take me to the slaughterhouses on the outskirts of Phoenix, where we'd buy up the little colts whose mothers had already had their throats slit. The babies would skit around the corral with wide-eyed fright, snorting through their nostrils, afraid to even let their hooves touch the ground. The feeling that hung in the air was sheer terror. I understood that instinctively, despite being so young, and the smell of death seeped through the car windows as we drove in the dusty lane leading back to the slaughter pens. Mom said that most horses here were stolen from farms and given to slaughter because of the foreigner's love of horse meat, and that was the first time that I knew that we were different. Because my God, Mom would say, who could ever eat a horse's meat?

* * *

My father pants like a puppy, hangs his tongue out. The bike wobbles and spits down the sidewalk, my training wheels freshly shucked. He runs alongside, hanging onto the back of the bike seat.

"You're doing it baby, *Go, Go*, pump the pedals."

His shout at my side fades as I take flight from the push of his palm, pedalling furiously down the sidewalk. Like my father, my tongue hangs out, my face frozen in studied concentration. My arms are bent with a death grip on the handlebars, *I'm riding my bike*! And I have left my father behind. The ends of my long hair blow off my back, the squares of concrete rush beneath me. But I want my father here, running alongside. I turn to find him and see him back at the house, a block away. I tap my toes to the sidewalk to stop and the bike shimmies. My foot catches in the frame and I topple over, skinning my knee, my hair tangling in the chain. I look to my father and scream but it's not the pain that brings hot tears. It's my dad talking to the neighbour, only stopping long enough to wave wildly for me to walk back to him.

That night, Dad pads down the hallway to the bathroom where I soak my knee in the tub. He rummages through the medicine cabinet for a hairgrip.

He sticks the curved end deep into his ear and scrapes, sinking his eyes closed.

"Honey, don't ever let me see you do this."

He jiggles the grip and looks at it, then presses it to the leg of his shorts, popping a crescent moon of burnt orange ear wax onto his leg.

"If you ever want to clean your ears, honey." He sticks the bobby pin back in the cabinet. "You come get either me or mommy. You never want to run a bobby pin in your ear without one of us there to supervise."

It was just after the first Christmas in Phoenix that the call came in from the base. Dad had tangled himself up while clearing out industrial drains and been spit out again, with both elbows snapped.

My father sits at the dinette in the kitchen, his casted arms folded to his chest like a mummy, anchored by double slings that criss-cross over him and tie around his neck. His fingers rest under his shoulders and look like garden grubs, curled black and blue.

Our mother forks three poached eggs from pan to plate, "Here, feed your father," she says and drops the plate on the table, walking out.

I butter his toast and spoon a bite of egg onto the corner. I stand at his knee and lift it to his mouth.

My father leans forward, armless. He bares his teeth and bites. A bit of yolk dribbles down his chin and I dab it with a napkin. The bottom rim of his eye wells, one giving way to a quiver.

34

"You're so good to me, baby." A tear splashes down his cheek.

I stand before my father, lift my small hands to his face. His drops his head into the cradle of my palms and I bear the weight of my father's heavy head.

"You're so good to your Daddy," he sobs.

"It's okay, Daddy."

"Will you take care of me, baby?"

"I'll take care of you, Daddy."

"I got nobody else but you."

He lifts his forehead from my hands.

"I love you so much, baby."

A tear drops from his chin to my face.

"I love you, too."

It trickles down and we are bonded; his tear in my eye, sealing me as my father's keeper.

With Dad at home in his slings, Mom tries another approach with Grandma Madge. We pick her up at her own crack jack house a mile away and drive to a pool party of one of the neighbours.

"Whatever you do Madge," Mom warns in the car, "for God's sake don't embarrass me."

I spotted her first when she stepped out of the changing cabana. My grandmother ran a band of long black hair from her belly button to her thighs and there it was in all its glory. When she spotted me and Mom across the patio at the bowl of chips, she waved over the heads of a pool of people, "Sannndy, Jeweeelly, over here!"

Mom walked straight in the front door that night and said, "Dan, I could have died."

When Dad's casts came off he returned to the base, only to find he no longer had a job. In the time he'd worked as a plumber, he'd racked up almost more time off with pay than he'd spent working.

And that's how we ended up leaving Phoenix, and back in Ohio, moving through a series of apartments and mobile homes in a never ending quest to be settled. I went to four different kindergartens alone; just making a new friend before being yanked out again. We finally spent six months in a rented trailer, long enough for Dad to till a garden and mound rows of dirt to plant cantaloupes. On Saturdays, he'd load great baskets of ripe melons into the back of the car and drive us over to the new base where he worked, parking at the edge of the gates to wait for the military men coming and going on shift. I sat on the tailgate of the family station wagon, swinging my legs, happy as a clam to be with my father. Dad was a master melon grower and the men of the base always pulled over to share a joke or a story with my dad and walk away with an armful of juicy cantaloupes. I watched them as the sun set and laughed with them, even though I didn't know what they talked about. But it was just the warmth of the people who sought out my father that I liked so much; men who smiled and laughed and didn't carry the weight and anger of my mother. And Dad was never like this when they were together. I experienced my parents separately – and it was my father who stole my heart.

And who knew that it would be in the hollow of Burns Road where we'd finally settle or that I'd come of age on the same track of isolation in which my life began? But we were driven to the ends of the earth by the 22 different jobs Dad had over the years and his increasing need for shelter, each loss a slit in the fabric of my father's well-being and an obvious indication that the world was conspiring against him. After all, the proof was all around us. Grandma Madge was crazy. Former bosses were crazy. The people who got him fired were crazy. The only one who was not mad, my father insisted and I wholeheartedly agreed, was him.

Chapter Three

I was ten and my little brother Daniel Joseph the third was only three that first year we moved down into the hollow. With no other children for miles and parents who didn't know the meaning of a play date, my brother and I were one another's best friends from the start. I loved him something fierce and called him by the variety of nicknames Dad had christened him with as a baby; *peanut* and then more specifically, *goober*. And little Danny, in his every effort to say Julie, called me "Dewey" or just "Sissy" for short.

We weave our little fingers together;

> *Here's the church.*
> *Here's the steeple.*
> *Open the door and here's all the people.*

When we open our palms, we wiggle our fingertips
to show all the "people". Me and Danny sit on the floor
of the trailer and hold our own church, led by the
fading remnants of Sunday school and a smathering
of tokens hard won there from memorizing verse;
Bible-shaped erasers and white pencils with psalms
embossed in gold; *Do unto others as you would have
them do unto you.*

Because I was seven years older than my brother, it was
my job to recall the memories of life before Burns
Road since that was all he could remember. My little
brother props his elbows on his knees, chin in hand
and listens intently to stories of paved roads for bicy-
cles, neighbourhood kids we could play with and the
first old car Dad bought when Danny was just a baby,
a 1920 Model A Ford we named Mr Hoover, that Dad
would take us out in on Sundays. The car only went
20 miles an hour but the thrill of climbing up into the
hard ribbed backseat and the ancient interior smell of
oil, gasoline and leather had Danny convinced he
could remember those afternoons crystal clear. Dad
had an orange triangle for slow-moving buggies he

rigged on the back and we'd pull out onto the road at a crawl. I held Danny on my lap and we'd peer through the open window, anxiously awaiting an oncoming car.

"Dad, Dad, do the ooga-ooga horn," I'd yell when I spotted one, and Dad would lock his arm straight and press hard the centre button of the steering column.

Ooooga-oooooooooga.

The other car would honk back and I'd hold baby Danny by the wrist and flap his hand to the driver as they smiled and drove past. Those Sunday afternoons we all had our hands out the windows as we crawled along the inside lane, waving to the cars that slowed down to admire us as we rolled on. I felt so special in the back of Mr Hoover, with my little brother on my lap, an ingrained sense of pride and ownership of them both.

Mom rarely went because the smell of the interior made her carsick and she had to keep her head on a swivel, she said, to watch out for cars that came up on us too fast. When she was there, by the time we were halfway through the drive, Dad was sulking at the wheel and we'd stopped waving out the window altogether.

Danny had just turned three when Mom made Dad sell Mr Hoover for the move to the country. It seemed as if our descent down the dirt road stripped us of the very thing that made us colourful out in the world. Without the car, we faded from view, Dad behind the wheel of a wide-body station wagon and two bored and bickering kids in the back.

Danny was too small to remember the cool car so he didn't know what he was missing. But Dad lived so vicariously through my little brother's Matchbox car collection, expounding big plans for the day he would build us our own classic car, that Danny became as obsessed with the idea of us getting one as I was nostalgic over the loss of the one we'd had.

The outside of our used trailer was dingy white and had interior features Mom referred to as "top of the line." Doorknobs and bathroom fixtures were cast in gold plastic, some with a marble swirl and little crank-out handles jutted from windows far too narrow to let the light of day in, let alone the tang out.

Our mother's rampant decorating saw us pasting up orange velvet wallpaper and painting accents with gold leaf on everything from the drain stopper to the little plastic clips that held the mirror to the bathroom wall. When the sink faucet she'd spraypainted silver began to fleck, we'd dab at it from a luminescent jar of my brother's model car paint. Bark art from the Circleville Pumpkin Show displayed a riveting image of *Tecumseh's Last Stand*, which was shellacked onto a slab of stained and charred wood and fitted with a toothy mount on the back, suitable for display. Needless to say, the trailer, and all that was in it, was rightfully Mom's domain. Tan press board was eventually sided up over the aluminium of the exterior and the shutters were drenched in chocolate brown paint.

My mother, wanting to give our trailer some European flair, ordered a plastic cuckoo clock from the back of *The Swiss Colony* catalogue and hung it next to the hutch that held my father's blue felt coin collecting books, to which the best years of pennies, nickels, dimes and quarters were pressed after being panned from a large clear plastic pretzel barrel that sat wedged in between the couch and the wall. The cuckoo clock chimed on the hour and two plastic birds, one blue, the other yellow, popped out a miniature barn door and circled on a track. The clock's long chains cascaded down the wall and moulded plastic pine cones dangled at the ends of them, inches above the carpet.

Just like Arizona, time was spent with either Mom or Dad, but rarely both. Even at Christmas, when my father parked in the living room to watch us open presents, Mom scurried through the trailer tending to forgotten tasks. It was as if a hotplate existed just underfoot and began to heat up whenever they landed in the same room together.

Only one photo exists of my father on Burns Road in his boyish state, taken just after we'd moved in. It is a picture of me, Danny, Dad and his two best buddies from the base where he worked. Rolly Polanka and Tommy Templeton were happy, good-natured men, just like my father. Always happy to see us and a joy to be around, they cracked jokes with Dad about gas and crap and never tired once of the same ones. Danny and I laughed just because they did. Excited in their company, we snuck up on the couch and jumped on their heads, rough housing with them for attention.

Life with my father is resurrected as much in memory of our place on Burns Road as it is in the pain found at the end of it. Our one-acre yard was a sea of brilliant lush grass that surrounded the trailer like a moat and I remember riding on a tractor mower in a lime green bikini, leaning into curves around weeping willow saplings, planted to give an air of permanence against the transience of our home. Yellow insulators hung on an electric fence and billowy seeds of milkweed drifted lazily in the summer breeze. A faded canvas halter tied up with baling twine hung just inside the tack shed, next to thick braided reins draped over rusty nails. The call of a lone bobwhite haunted the early summer dusk when I'd pad out in my bare feet and lock the shed doors to keep the raccoons out. A rusty horseshoe dug from the loose earth was haphazardly balanced over the mouth of my father's garage, a treacherous structure at the edge of the driveway he had cobbled together with twelve-foot-long pieces of rusted sheet metal nail gunned over rough frame.

The garage itself was a dark maze of car parts, milk crates overflowing with a jumble of tools, hand saws and claw hammers dangling from hooks overhead. And back in the dimmest, eeriest corner, in a place no child or budding teenage girl would ever willingly wander, lurked my father's long metal workbench. The solo fluorescent light that lit his cave buzzed like a fly zapper from where it hung by a dog chain from the low ceiling to shine a five-foot radius on the concrete floor. But even on the brightest of summer days, there were parts of this creepy edifice that remained pitch black.

Our hollow held the kind of raw beauty a band of wild hill children might – shy and innocent, but you could never quite trust them. You weren't scared of the woods down on Burns Road; you were scared of who might be in there with you.

With the passing of each season, memories of civilization faded and life dwindled to a crawl. Where once I hummed songs from the Sunday schools we used to go to, the lines and eventually the chorus were washed over by the jingles of toy commercials that rang through the trailer on any given Sunday's worth of television: *Mon-chi-chi-Mon-chi-chi, oh so soft and cuddly* my pretty po-nee, she gives me so much love *Weebles wobble, but they don't fall down.* Danny and I strung them back to back, changing key and pitch to mimic the TV as Dad clicked through the three country channels again and again and again, waiting for a new rerun to start.

By the time I was twelve, my father had grown to be one with his chair, plopping down in it from the time he came home from work until well after the late evening news. And, although I knew where he was physically, I couldn't for the life of me find the dad I once felt so close to. He was still happy to see me when he walked through the door but, once he sat in his chair, efforts to reach him were futile. When I could, I'd sit on the couch for hours just to be there should he wish to talk to me. But he didn't. I would rack my brain, *think, think*, trying to come up with something that might turn his attention from the television set. But the parting of my mouth, sensed out of the corner of his eye, would elicit a shush or be met by the swish of a forefinger in the air as he winced, leaning forward to piece together what he might have missed. As a last resort, I watched with him, anchored to whatever time we could have together. But even though I didn't have the right things to say, I believed with all my heart that if I could find the secret words or right way to be, I could unlock the mystery and win back my father. We were so close when he broke his arms, surely I could find a way to resurrect our bond.

"Who's the King?"

"You are, Dad!"

"Who's the King in this house?"

"Dad is!" Danny and I ring in unison.

"That's right. I'm King and you better obey."

My father cackles with good nature while my brother and I disperse from the end of the couch to carry out orders. Dad's throne was his La-Z-Boy chair and the food that piled up around it – corn nuts, pork rinds, almost empty boxes of popcorn, bags of corn chips – was the gold on his altar. The empties surrounded him like gilded gifts to be fingered when he needed reminding of his total reign. His was the authority to yell from the seat of his throne and have anything within a five-hundred foot radius delivered to him, without complaint and with total servitude by us kids.

"Fix me some toast Sissy, would you? I want the good jelly, not any of that marmalade shit your mother gets."

And I would drop whatever I was doing and trot off to make the toast, trying extra hard to get it right.

Our mother, with her ears like a bat, never missed a chance to pot shot him.

"That's right, Dannnn," her voice spat from somewhere beyond the thin wall of the living room. "Turn the kids into your niggers. Make them wait on you hand and foot."

"You just go back to whatever you were doing, *Dingbat*," my father would shout, then turn his head to snigger at us, his face scrunched up like a little boy and we'd snigger back, because we knew no better.

If our mother was at least two rooms away, Dad called her the names of the wives and hated mother-in-laws he picked up from television sit-coms – *Dingy, Dingbat, Dummy* – all gauged by how thin her voice was as it hammered through the panelling. Otherwise, if she yelled from the open kitchen behind his chair, he squirmed from the embarrassment of being caught and fiddled with the remote.

I didn't mind running for Dad. The errands were usually quick and painless and he responded with exaggerated thrill to receive the fetched item – often making it into a game.

"Let's see how fast you can run out to the car, Sissy, and get me the bag of gumdrops on the seat. If they ain't there, check the floor. Okay … ready, set, go!"

"Whoa, you did that in 60 seconds?" he'd shout when I returned breathless with the bag. "Way to go, Sis!"

It was only on the rarest of occasions when we were lucky enough to be left at home with our father and without Mom around, that a bit of the veil would lift, lightness would blow in the skinny windows and trailer life didn't seem so bad.

My father bellows out the kitchen patio door. Danny and I hold hands and jump from the deck into the gem green water of the pool, flourescent from the double cups of chlorine we dump in at random to clean it.

"Don't you guys go pee-pee in there."

"Dad!" I shout, "That's gross!" But I can see my little brother, soaking to his neck in the water like a little snow monkey. "Danny!"

Home alone with our father, we are just kids. When Mom goes to town on a shopping trip, she claims our time with a list of chores to do before she gets home. We follow her to the car, faces drawn. But as soon as she rounds the first bend, Danny and I run in the trailer and shriek down the hall to change into our bathing suits.

My father slaps his hands together in jubilation, "When the cat's away, the mice will play!"

He loads up a ham sandwich with sweet pickles in the kitchen and, as we run past, we beg him to watch us dive off the deck into the pool.

"Dad, Dad, Look!" I dunk my brother, who lurks just under the surface ready to spring up on my shoulders and push me under.

Dad stands on the porch in his stocking feet and cut-off jean shorts and waves to us with a mouth full of food. He trumpets his nose on the hem of his shirt then pins one nostril with his finger, blowing the rest out. It bolts like a slash against the side skirt of the trailer, painted tan to coordinate with the plastic brown shutters. I can see it from the edge of the pool, where I hook my elbows over the side to watch my father.

"You kids have fun, I'll be in the garage if you need me."

"Dad, Dad, can we listen to some of your records?"

"Yeah, Sissy, put on *Sergeant Pepper*!"

I was eight, and the trailer was still in my future, when I first discovered the coolness of my father's extensive record collection. I lay on the floor after school, bobbing my feet above me, panning through the long stack of albums leaned up against the wall, relegated to the one room in the house that Mom let him keep his things. At first I pulled out all the albums with the cool covers but there was only one I listened to all the way through: *Sergeant Pepper's Lonely Hearts Club Band*.

The Beatles were my father's favourite band and John Lennon was his hero. If we were lucky enough in the car to catch *Hey Jude* on the radio, my father would stretch his arm back over the seat and wiggle his fingers for me to hold his hand. He sang through the verses, growing ever more melancholy. As the song neared its end, I would catch my father looking at me in the rear view mirror, his eyes glassy with tears.

"Sing it with me, baby. *Na, na, na, nananana, nananana, Hey Jude.*"

I leaned forward to sing along with my father and saw in the mirror that a tear had run down his face. He squeezed my hand as his cheeks grew shiny, his voice cracking in song. A lump rose in my throat and I could feel my own tears falling down my face. I held my father's hand as tight as I could and laid my wet face against it, showing alliance. I did not know why I cried or even what the song was about, but such was the power of my father's tears.

Now that we're stuffed into a trailer with no extra room, Dad's record collection has been delegated to the last tiny corner left. The only time a record of Dad's gets on the turntable is when Mom is gone; otherwise she says it's the devil's music.

I run in the house dripping wet and lug one of the big stereo speakers all the way out the patio door to the

51

edge of the deck. I dry my hands and carefully place the record on the turntable, making sure to only hold the album between thumb and forefinger, and lower the needle ever so delicately as Dad has shown me. Then I crank up the volume. The crazy calliope guitar of the first song on the *Sergeant Pepper* album hits the still air and we know it can't be heard for a country mile.

The sun beats down on my tan shoulders and I bask in a plastic tube chaise longue in the yard, painting my toenails, bobbing my head to the beat. Danny mock sings on the deck of the pool, using an inflatable duck ring as a microphone. He jumps off sideways and a great tsunami wave careens over the side. Life is good. But even better than the rock and roll booming through the yard on a country summer Saturday, is knowing that Dad is listening right along with me all the way in the garage.

At the first sign of fall, my stomach drops. Pressed Wranglers lie stiff on my bed, paired with back-to-school tops from K-Mart. The impending first day of school brings with it a flurry of anxiety as spiral notebooks and ring binders are picked out with painstaking care, knowing that one false move could destroy your entire year. If you pick the Hang in There, Kitty and everybody else has the pack of galloping horses, you might as well forget it.

"Kids are cruel, honey," my father pep talks me as I cry in frustration. "And if you opened your eyes, you'd see that half of the school is making fun of you behind your back. You don't need those kids. Stick with Daddy, I'll be your friend."

And for a moment things don't seem so bad.

Mom takes her fork and perforates another slice of pumpkin pie. The pan is dotted with black lava-like bubbles of carbonized pie juice after being baked at a scorching heat.

She unbuttons her trousers, the pink skin of her belly rushing down her zipper like a flashflood. Mom throws down her fork in a huff. "Dan, you shouldn't have let me eat so much. God, I'm stuffed."

I sit on the couch in the living room while my father tips back ninety degrees in his chair. He looks over and rolls his eyes. He flicks a chunk of black crust off his own piece of pie and whispers in conspiracy, "I don't know why your mother has to fucking cook everything on high."

Early in life we had to develop a taste for our mother's tendency to scorch food, and to eat of its ruin without flinching – crispy spaghetti, seared chilli and rubbery hot dogs permanently watermarked from being boiled on high for an hour.

"Jesus, Julie, look what you made me do, talking to me when I'm trying to cook, taste this – is it scorched?" and she'd shove a spoonful of charred chilli to my lips.

"No, it's good, Mom, you can't taste the scorch at all."

It's best to lie to my mother, with her quick hands that strike like lightning. A brutal woman, with nothing gentle, romantic or mysterious about her, she would backhand me in the grocery store and bloody my nose, then walk off with the cart leaving me to feel embarrassed like it was my fault. So we ate our crisp salmon patties moulded out of a can of fish and an egg without gripe or complaint, quietly pressing the soft cylinder bones to the roofs of our mouths until they burst.

At school, I bummed quarters from the kids in my class to buy potato chips and snack cakes but on the weekend I was left to fend for myself inside the dank avocado-coloured refrigerator, overstocked with a mixture of stale meat soaking in its own blood, expired dairy products and vegetables left in there so long they had turned to algae in their respective produce bags. Any hunk of cheese I discovered came with its own layer of green mould.

"Just cut it off," Dad would yell from his chair when I'd protest. "Hell, that's all cheese is anyway, *good mould*."

I'd rummage through to find the only item safe enough to eat: single-sliced, individually wrapped, processed American cheese. Even if there was some kind of dripping or weird indistinguishable smear on the plastic, it still meant this cheese was sealed for my protection. I'd peel the sticky wrapper off and voila, the perfect food.

My brother and I lay our torn-off pieces of cheese on stale tortilla chips and microwaved on high. We cracked the molten shape of cheesy chips off the paper plate and broke it into equal shares and were left to scrap for bits of petrified cheese sunken into the grooves of the paper plate. It did not matter if there was a bit of paper melded in; this was still a breakfast of champions.

Besides, Mom's cooking was worse than faring for ourselves in the refrigerator or navigating the greasy orange interior of the microwave. A staple at her dinner table was chipped beef on toast made from packets of lunch meat. Stirred with lumpy gravy, our mother cooked it on high until it was scorched to a brown paste, then scooped it out onto toast we had to decarbonize by scraping the black off with the edge of a butter knife.

Breakfast was even worse. Mom would whip up an industrial-sized box of powdered milk, pour it into empty plastic milk jugs – still with a milk ring curdled sour around the rim – and stick them out in the 40-cubic-foot freezer in the garage.

When we ran out of milk, we would have to lug out one of these frozen ice blocks from the freezer depths and let it thaw on the counter. With the half-thawed milk floating in the jug like an iceberg, Mom would pour the thin liquid over breakfast. Our Saturday morning bowls of exciting cereals – the Sugar Smacks and Fruity Pebbles we'd begged for so laboriously in the supermarket aisles – now sat lifeless in their watery tombs. We spooned them to our lips with trepidation, the magic of the commercials long gone.

But when Dad snapped his chair upright and said, "Get me the mitts," excitement filled the air.

"Dad's cooking!" Danny barrelled down the hall, shouting at the top of his lungs. I'd run back down with him, equally overjoyed and we'd stand attentive as Dad gussied up in preparation to turn the stove burner on.

Dad was the best cook – even if it was like prodding a large slothful animal with an electric zapper to prize him out of his chair long enough to get him to the kitchen. But when we did, it was magic. Suddenly, in my father's hands, food became edible and delicious. There was not a film, rind or fleck of black carbon you had to remove from your dish before you could put it in your mouth. There was not a cluster of strands from our mother's hairpiece to pick off your tongue. You just forked up the food, thought nothing of it and ate.

Granted, we had to stay in the kitchen with our father and do nearly everything except stand at the pan. But it was worth it. We'd beg him to make his special spaghetti recipe and he'd sprinkle sugar in the sauce. We'd beg him to make bacon-and-egg sandwiches, and he'd sprinkle sugar on the bacon as it sizzled in the skillet.

Everything my father touched turned golden and delicious. When we ate we did so with rapture, urgency, as if we could not remember the last time we did so and did not know when food like this would ever come again. There were never leftovers. When my father cooked, I squirrelled away every last thing he made. It was the only material proof of him I could take with me.

My father sits in a cloud of his own gas. Mom stands at the kitchen counter, rolling pin in one hand, the other cocked and loaded, a dusting of flour on her hip.

"For God's sake, Dan, would you get up off your lazy ass and give me a hand in here?"

A tuft of my father's hair pokes from over the top of the La-Z-Boy, his back to the open kitchen. A commercial is on.

"I told you, Sandy, when a commercial comes on."

My father sneezes cataclysmically; everything exists for him large.

My brother does a proper table setting, circling round and round the table, setting our cheap flattened silverware on picnic napkins as carefully as if they were damask.

We all sit down to say grace. Dad scratches his head with the prongs of an up-flipped fork.

"Dear heavenly Father," he starts.

Mom flicks my wrist with her finger, "Stop smacking your lips or I'm gonna smack them for you." Her eyes still closed in prayer.

Dad continues, "We thank you for this delicious food. Amen."

"I want to know, Dann," Mom starts, "when you're going to get the addition built on? I've been hounding you for what, I don't know, eight months now? We're running out of room for my stuff."

"Sandy, you don't need to be buying any more clothes." And it was true. Mom had so many shoes she had bought a horse trailer, parked it in the yard and begun throwing in black bin bags of shoes until they were piled to the top.

"It's not just my stuff, it's the kids' shit and your shit too."

"If you stopped buying it, we wouldn't need more room to put it."

Mom follows Dad from the kitchen as he plops in his chair, Danny and I clear the table, clanking dishes into the sink. Mom positions herself across from the TV.

"If you wouldn't mind, I'd just be tickled pink, you know? I mean, I wouldn't know how to act, if you would just for one fucking second talk to me. Communicate."

My father hiccup-belches. "What do you want to talk about?"

"Anything!"

"Can we do it later? I'm letting my food digest."

I pinch off a lug of cheese in the fridge and soften it in my fingers, roll it into a ball.

"Later never comes, Dannnn. We have got to talk now, pronto. If we're going to stay married, you have got to talk to me like man and wife."

My father shifts in his chair.

"Are you listening to me?"

He tucks his hands between his legs.

"Godammit, Dan, I'm talking to you!"

He laughs at a commercial.

"You motherfucking rotten son of a bitch," Mom screams, "How dare you ignore me to watch the same commercial you've seen a million times."

"Sandy, leave me alone, will ya? We don't need to talk about anything."

"Oh, we don't, huh? We don't have to talk about what a loser you are? Or how you can't keep a job? Or that your kids don't respect you? Or how you sit there night after night like a lump on a log? Yeah, right," Mom snorts, "You're crazier than I thought."

My father grips the side handle. "I don't have to take this shit," he shouts, and jettisons from the chair. But Mom tries to block him and they scuffle at the door. He knocks her against the hutch and crashes out of the house.

"Dad!" I yell from after him, "Where are you going?"

"I'm going to hell, Julie." He storms off the deck. "Straight to hell."

"Julie, you can count your friends on the fingers of one hand." Mom holds up a few fingers, demonstrating. "I do and do and do for people and here I am, 39, and what do I got to show for it? Nothing!"

Mom hyperventilates into a brown paper bag. In between breaths she takes a silver table spoon from the freezer and presses its curved back to the swollen puffs of her eyelids.

The fights that started in the trailer and ended when Dad stormed out often saw Mom chasing down the road after him in the spare car. She'd return alone later that night, her red face red streaked with tears.

"Julie, let me tell you something," she says. "The one you love at 20 is not the one you love at 30."

The kind of crying Mom did lasted hours and by morning her eyelids were nearly swollen shut. She'd splash water on her face, compress a cold washcloth to her eyes or scrub on kohl eye liner but it just made her look like a raccoon. The only thing that reduced the swelling was a tablespoon from the silverware drawer run under the cold tap and stuck in the freezer until it froze into a thin, rounded ice cube. She would corner me in the kitchen and stand by the counter with the cold curve of the spoon pressed into the hollow of her eye socket. I leaned against the refrigerator, my hands tucked behind me, sliding them up and down the smooth wood-grain sticker she'd applied to the silver handle.

"Does it look better now?" she'd ask as she lifted the spoon from her eye. It didn't.

"Uh, a little bit."

"How about now?" she'd say, raising it again, her eyeball popping up.

"Maybe a few more minutes."

I vacillated wildly between first feeling sorry for my father and then Mom. I hated how she cornered him but I would show alliance to her even as she called him vicious names. I shared an understanding with Dad but hearing Mom sob through the night and seeing her face the morning after, I couldn't help but feel sorry for her. What Mom feared most was Dad walking out and no longer being the breadwinner. She painted a bleak picture of life without his pay cheque; no more shopping, no horses, no nice knick-knacks ordered from the catalogues to set around the trailer – all things our mother wanted that didn't really matter to me. But I was scared when she said she'd have to pull us out of school to live in a shelter for homeless women and if that didn't work, give us up to foster care. Mom would turn on her best behaviour to win Dad back, but once the threat was over, she unleashed a vengeance for her dependency that cast darkness over our family for weeks. And when Dad lost another job, the cycle of regular fights accelerated to almost daily shouting matches over money.

"Dan, what are we going to do? I can't pay the mortgage."

"Let them take the fucking place, I'll go live in the garage."

"And what about us?" Mom seethed. "You expect your kids to live in that filthy rat trap with you?"

"They can if they want to," Dad reasoned.

* * *

In the weeks that followed my father's last pay cheque, Mom was supposed to budget to stretch out the money but instead went on rampant shopping sprees, buying up the outfits she had her eye on. The cheques bounced at the bank and piled up with fees and penalties and Mom, in a dramatic display of righteous indignation, would stand at the window of a teller and bang her fist on the counter trying to get the charges reversed until they escorted her out.

As for Dad, he never saw a dime from his pay cheques anyway. The only thing he had that was of any importance was his record collection.

But without the money to fuel Mom's fantasy, her world tipped on its axis and rolled straight down to crash into my father's.

Mom's hair is a wild windstorm of stray hairs that stick out from the jet-black hairpiece she has wound up into a cone on top of her head. She stomps through the kitchen, slamming plates down on gold-flecked Formica.

"You go tell that good for nothing, son of a bitchin, no good motherfucking father of yours, *Dannnn*, that his dinner is ready."

"Hey, Dad," I sing-song, approaching the dark lair of the garage, "Mom says she's fixed up your favorite dinner. She'd love for you to come in and eat with us."

I hold my breath, staring into the black abyss of the garage. I can just make out my father's shadow, stooped on a milk crate sorting through the junk under his workbench.

"*Please*, Daddy."

"Well, you go tell your mother that she can just kiss my rosy fucking ass, will you?" he shouts. "It's going to take more from that lunatic than her slop to get me to step back inside that hell-hole."

"Okay." And I crunch back down the gravel walkway.

"Dad said he'll be in in a few minutes, he's gotta finish what he's doing and clean up. He said to tell you that he loves you, *Mommy*."

Back and forth, lobbing my own lies, rinsing the filth from theirs, until five to six trips later Dad reluctantly opens the aluminium screen door and tromps back down the hall to soap his hands with a goop of orange hand cleaner.

He looms like a giant at the yellow plastic vanity, with its dainty shell soap dishes scalloped right into the sink. He shakes his hands off on the fake marble of the counter, peppering the mirror. Dirty froth and water streak down the bowl and pool on the counter. Dad stomps out, turning down the hall and I slip in, wiping the basin clean with the guest towel and rinsing the dirt down the drain. I toss the towel into the long cabinet behind my mother's wigs and pads and the secret stash of *Frederick's of Hollywood* catalogues she orders them from. I mean, who's going to use a guest towel in our house?

The threat of divorce hung in the air thick as burning bacon and was a constant force being prepared for in various forms of execution. Mom made a big production of having us load clothes into a paper sack and keep it in the back of our closets for anytime she thought we may need to flee under cover of night. That she announced it loudly while pacing in front of Dad and the TV seemed to defy the intended secrecy of it all, but we followed orders.

And after dinner when she railed on him as he lay beached in the chair, my brother and I sat cross-legged on the floor in the back of the trailer as we once did playing church. But this time we were perfectly still, straining our ears for the recliner footrest to snap shut. If it did, we'd have to bolt to the living room and get between them in their physical fight. Every shout or stomp ricocheted though the trailer and vibrated the glass panels of the hutch, so just as Dad read Mom's proximity to him by the strength of her voice through the walls, we read the levity of their arguments by the needle on our own internal Richter scale. There was no way to stop them and just as you'd think Dad's attention might make Mom back off, it only fuelled a desire to make him pay.

"What do you want me do to Sandy?" my father would plead, "I'll do anything just to get you to stop. Stop, Sandy, I'm begging you to stop."

My father stands trapped in the vortex of the trailer where the living room, hallway and kitchen all meet. He keeps his eye on the front door but Mom blocks the exit, her arm strung out, gripping the edge of the hutch.

"Dan, you are going to stand here, face me like a man and deal with this."

My father sighs.

Mom cuts, "Stop acting like a little boy, Dannn. I want to be married to a man."

Danny and I sneak down the hall to stand guard.

Mom and Dad wedge into the tiny archway opening, my father's face dropped in defeat. Mom reads our presence as allies and edges in.

"C'mon, Dannn," she taunts, "What are you going to do? Huhhhh?"

"I'm begging you, Sandy," my father says quietly, "Please leave me alone."

"What!" Mom mocks, "I can't hear you little boy, going to stand there and cry?"

Mom points to us crouched in the hallway. "The kids aren't going to help you, are you kids? They're here because they know how crazy you are."

"Please Sandy, please let me go." My father looks up from his hand, exasperated. Mom leers with a smirk, "You're going have to talk louder if you want me to hear you."

"Mom," I whisper. "Please."

He can beg, we can beg but she will not stop.

Her smile fades, "You son of a bitch." And she gains steam, "You rotten, good for nothing son of a fucking bitch! I do and do and do and do for you and what do I get? You got nothing here, you destroyed this home. I hate you, these kids hate you."

Danny squeaks, "We don't hate you, Dad."

"We love you both," I plead.

We emerge from the shadows; Danny latches onto the seam running down my father's jean leg, I slip in against my mother's hip, placing myself between them. Mom sneers like a heckler in his face, Dad holds his head in his hands inches from her spitting mouth. Pressed against Mom, I can feel my father's rage building. With a sudden flare his head jerks upright. His fists shoot out of nowhere and he rushes, tangling his hands in her hair, smacking her gutted mouth. He catches her jaw in the crook of his palm, gripping her cheeks. She folds her chin to her chest like a child being tickled.

My father squeezes.

"Helllp! Heeelp me Juwelly, Denny." Mom's eyes are as wide as golf balls, pleading over the top of my father's hand.

"Let her go!" I screech.

"Call her off, Julie," Dad screams, "Make her leave me alone!"

"I will, Dad, I promise, I'll make her stop!"

Dad shoves her from his grip; she crashes into the crevice of the couch, separating it from the wall. The pretzel barrel tips and coins spill like a jackpot over my father's feet. He heaves his foot out of the pile to haul back and kick her and I desperately tug the belt loops of my mother's Gloria Vanderbilt jeans, trying to pull her from the slit of the sofa. Dad's drawn boot hits the wall, tangling in the chains of the clock, a pine cone whips around his ankle. He catches himself against the hutch as heirloom mail-order plates crash from their plastic holders. The clock flies off the wall, crashing at my mother's feet. My brother rips from his death grip on the seam of my father's pants and crumples to the floor, crying. We break in the swirling vortex of the trailer, catching our breath. The jostled hands strike the hour and the little birds pop out the door of the clock, lying on its side, *Cuckoo! Cuckoo!*, they circle on the track.

* * *

School was full of kids whose parents were divorced and returned to class with stories of fun-filled weekends spent with either their mom or dad. I envied them. The only reason my parents fought was because they were together. Instead of getting the best of them like the kids of divorced parents, we got the worst of both. We could handle being with one or the other so the only thing stopping the harmony was the fact that they would not split. But while together, Danny and I lived each day with antennas tuned to the brewing of fights that ran in cycles day by day. And they always ended by the same formula; Dad taking off in the car with Mom in hot pursuit, or Dad pummelling Mom until she finally grew silent.

Despite us begging and pleading, cornering them separately or tag teaming them together, the sweet relief of divorce never came. My brother and I sat in one bedroom or the other, secretly plotting how happy our lives would be if only for the love of God they would just separate. Danny cries bitter tears, his lip buckling under the weight. He cannot stand the fighting, the shuffling back and forth between Mom and Dad to smooth them out, the way they pit us against each other and force us to take sides. We focus instead on the future and talk with excitement about the good times to be had once we are with just one of them. Mom or Dad, but never them both. Please, God, we pray together in our pyjamas on the floor in the dark, please never them both.

The only good thing that came of the fighting was the sporadic new beginnings Dad insisted would lead to a happy home life. Convinced all would be forgiven if we just attended church, Dad donned his blister-making shoes and Mom had a legitimate reason to try on half her outfits. We headed out early Sunday morning for one of the small country tabernacles that dotted the dirt roads throughout the county, the car ride heavy with tension.

I pop a bubble.

"Quit it!" My father chucks his fist into the backseat, swinging it like a pendulum. "Knock it off before I knock your block off."

He brakes for a curve and Mom sucks in a scream, bracing her hand against the dash.

"Dan, you're driving like a fucking maniac."

"Shut up! I'm trying to think."

The car goes quiet again; Mom and Dad resigning themselves to a ceasefire only possible if neither one opens their mouth. Once inside the church, I could finally separate from the family to sit with the other kids my age.

Dappled light filtered through the high stained-glass windows and dust motes speckled in what could only be God's own shine beaming down upon us. We

raised our voices to the rafters and soldiered out in
Sunday class:

Mine eyes have seen the glory of the coming of the Lord!
He is trampling out the vintage where the grapes of
wrath are stored!
He hath loosed the fateful lighting of His terrible swift
sword!
His truth is marching on!

Disguised in the masses, I shout the verses at the top of
my lungs. Church is the one place I can scream.

Chapter Four

I could not know it then, but just as country living had turned me gun shy around kids my own age, the isolation had also taken its toll on my father. Gone was society's delicate system of checks and balances, the fine line that divides the polite from the anti-social.

By the time I turned 14, there were no rules left for how Dad interacted with the outside world. He'd mumble "jackass" or "imbecile" in public just under his breath to complete strangers he didn't like the look of. He screeched cock-eyed into disabled parking spots, taking up a full space and slicing off the corners of the other two that flanked either side. My father shot his fist out the open window to flip off a driver, then hawked at their car if they even so much as looked at him.

"See that Meineke Muffler shop?" he'd point out as we drove past. "Watch out for them, they'll screw you with your pants on."

And I would peer in close at perfectly normal people going about their business and make a note never to go near them. "It's just us against them," Dad would say. "Your old man's got his head on a swivel. Stick with me, you'll be alright. Nobody's going to catch me with my pants down." There was no reason not to believe Dad. Who else was in my life? The bus ride to school was a lonely hour of being jostled on back roads in the pre-dawn and, once there, my days were spent mostly alone, scuttling from locker to class to bathroom, to check my hair in the mirror and try to make it less obvious how truly unpopular I was. My school was nestled amongst cornfields in one of the poorest counties in the state. Qualifying as parents was as much as making sure shoes were stuck on kids before sending them out the door. Dad didn't attend parent-teacher nights and, even whatever he would have told my teacher, they wouldn't have batted an eyelid. There's a reason people live that far out; a healthy suspicion of just about anything was rule of thumb.

When distant laughter erupted behind us in public, my father would whip around to find its source then turn back with a scowl on his face, "I'm sorry you had to hear that, honey."

I would look at the people.

"Them jerks are laughing at you, they don't care if they hurt your feelings or not. You stick with me, honey, I'll watch out for you."

And I learned from my father just how sneaky people can be. Without him as my watchdog, I never would have known how many people made fun of me.

When Dad was doing 75 miles an hour and we missed our connecting highway turn-off, he'd slam on the brakes, bellow *"Hang on, kids"* and take us off road, our one-tonne truck barrelling down the grassy slope with Dad flashing the lights at the oncoming cars on the highway below. Danny and I braced our palms against the dash, elbows locked open, eyes squeezed tight, *ahhhhh's* coming out bumpy as they were wash-boarded from our throats. As we careened closer to the bottom of the hill and the highway he wanted to be on, Dad would accelerate and we'd go crashing out over the gravel shoulder and into the empty lane, the cars below having watched us free fall from the highway above hugging the fast lane to get out of our way. We were rebels without a cause, running from a threat that didn't exist. It was like living in a real live *Dukes Of Hazard* episode; Crazy Cooter comin' at 'ya!

* * *

Dad had just landed a new job at the Sherex Chemical Company in Columbus, working as the building's sole maintenance man and driving alone an hour and a half each way to work. The company set him up in a makeshift office in the basement of their impressive mirrored high-rise, and Dad did whatever job came his way to help the building run smoothly. When an emergency water break or electrical crisis called him in over the weekend, I'd tag along and roller skate around the concrete floor of the basement, stepping in and out of the wood-framed corner my father worked from – which didn't even have walls or anything brighter than a low-wattage desk light. The radio echoed hollowly through the vast corridors and the feeling was suffocating as the floors above bore down on the exposed steel beams. Roller skating through the basement was fun for about ten minutes, then a feeling of complete and utter loneliness set in. I couldn't imagine spending the day there and would think of any excuse to roll into the elevator and find my father in the building above.

When Dad came home after a day of solitary confinement, crawling out the wormhole of silence proved too much. If driven from his chair by Mom's need to talk, he retreated to the back of the garage for the rest of the night.

The change in his thinking came so subtly that it was hard to see the forest for the trees. But slowly, the edges of my father's reality began to blur; suspicious thought outweighed reason until the remains of what was once his well-tempered personality was the tip of a rock and dark water lapped at the sides. Sometimes I could climb up on the precipice of the remaining edge and pull my father back, talking softly and peppering facts into the conversation, but mostly I was underwater with him, drowning, drowning.

Padding out to the garage to check his barometer, Dad peered in close at my T-shirt, showing a boy's face on an old fashioned TV set.

"Does your shirt say *Leave it to Beaver*?"

"That's the name of the show, that sit-com from the 1950s, don't you remember watching it?" The show ran for a decade and chronicled the innocent American life of a ten-year-old boy and his family.

"Who you trying to fool? Nobody's going to believe that!" Dad looked at me like I was pulling a fast one. "Don't you know what a beaver is? People think you're selling sex when you wear something like that."

And I walked away feeling gross, wondering how people could think that.

Out in public, we tag-teamed long enough to get back home. Dad steered me away from what wasn't good for me and I, intrinsically sensing my father's delicate disposition, began to shelter him in the same way. We were in a three-legged-race together, each bound to the other, hobbling through life, neither of us free. I hid behind my father to avoid the pain of not having friends and he hid behind me to ease his fears of an encroaching world. Looking back, I don't think we had any idea what had happened to us, but we were each scared of the same thing: people. And the isolation of our life together gave me blind faith in my father, so blind it undermined my own sense of reality.

"Sissy, get your shoes on," Dad hollered from the living room. "We're going to town."

My mind raced trying to come up with something to talk about for the long drive to the city. Where once we could occupy the car without the need for words, I now knew that every blank moment that slipped by carried with it the potential weight of Dad losing control.

The last time we hadn't said anything on the way to Columbus, we'd pulled into a McDonald's drive-thru for lunch. As I looked over the menu to order, a homeless man wandered up to ask for change. Lighting fast, my father folded his gun from his front pocket. "Fucking nigger," Dad said, whipping it out the window into the man's face. A shot of adrenaline surged through the car as Dad's other hand flipped the safety latch off.

"I'll blow your motherfucking head off!" he screamed.

78

It happened so fast.

The man's face froze, his eyes drawn to the gun.

"Dad, it's okay," I cried. And then calmer, "He didn't know. He's going to go now." My heart raced as my father pulled the gun back in, never taking his eyes off the man.

"You better run." Sweat ran down Dad's face.

"Yeah, I'll take a Big Mac and a diet," Dad said into the speaker. I can't remember if I ordered.

Every car ride since came with a built-in urgency to tap into my father's thoughts and counter them if necessary. I was the jukebox to his dime, selecting just the right record to set the mood; jitterbug to lift a cloud of anger, love song to help him cry. Either way, whether I was heading off an explosion or wrapping his neediness around me like a well-worn cloak, I was tuned in to my father.

I stared out the window *think, think*, the cornfields whizzing by; their golden tassels sturdy as soldiers. My father's one hand gripping the wheel, the other twisted around to rest over his gun in the front pocket of his trousers. His jaw flexed off and on like a warning light.

"Hey, Dad, I know. Let's play name that tune."

I scanned the radio, desperate.

Dad had stopped listening to music altogether; ever since he came home after work to the smell of burning plastic in the trash pit. I don't know if he knew by the white haze that hung over the driveway or the look on my face when he walked through the door but he dashed through the living room, desperate to find his records. I followed, helpless.

Our mother's new doll collection sat in the corner. Dolls ordered from tacky gift catalogues sent to the trailer; dolls in calico frocks and white billowy pantaloons, with black hair, brown hair, blond hair and strawberry hair. Dolls that Mom had been stock-piling in her closet until she decided to set them out on display. And the place she chose to do it was Dad's corner, the one his records were stacked in.

My father stormed out the front door and crunched down the gravel walkway, me close on his heels. I reached for his fingers, but sensing me behind him, he jerked them away before I could reach.

"I'm sorry, Dad. I didn't do it."

"I know, but you were in charge. I look out for you but what? You can't watch out for me?"

"I got off the bus and the dolls were sitting there. I didn't know it was the records until I saw them."

He stood at the edge of the fire pit, kicking through ash, the toe of his steel-toed boot turning over edges of singed album covers.

"That's all I had, Sissy," my father said, his eyes fixed on glowing embers.

"I'm sorry, Dad." And I was. Because neither of my parents took responsibility for anything, I absorbed the blame for everything. I kicked myself for letting it happen. If only I could have known, I'd have hid them under my bed.

"I got nothing now, Sissy. When you snooze, you lose."

I stood by my father at the edge of the trash pit, the air thick with the choke of black plastic. Gone was the Chubby Checker *Twist* album with the collectible stickers on the inside sleeve. The same one I had coveted in my room when I was only nine and peeled the pictures of an overweight twisting Chubby to arrange in a heart design on my school table. My father stood in the doorway of my bedroom when I excitedly showed him my work of art and choked out, "Baby, let's not do that to any more of Daddy's albums, okay?"

Dad knelt down and hot touched his fingers to the ash, registering what he had lost. At the edge of the fire pit, I spotted the hard plastic square from the cover of the *Sergeant Pepper's Lonely Heart Club Band* album, with John Lennon sitting cross-legged in a wizard's hat. Partly melted and grossly wavy, I picked its corner from the rubble and offered it to my father but he just turned away.

"That's all I had, Sis," he whispered, than faded into the garage.

I have always tried to make it up to him.

Familiar notes come on the radio and I stop the scanner. I couldn't have asked for better luck. It's the song I memorized by ear in the third grade when I first fell in love with my father's music. I waited for him by the door after work and asked him about the lyrics I couldn't make out. He placed the record on the turntable and cleared his throat, then sang in a voice that turned him into a poet. I watched mesmerized and wished someday I would have the courage to sing it with him. Each day after that I practised on the bus, marking the ride to school by the 14 minutes it took to sing the verses start to finish.

I have not heard it with him since.

"Hey, Dad, we know this one, don't we?"

My father smiles, whets his lips.

A long, long, time ago.

And he is suddenly happy.

And I can still remember how that music used to make me smile.

He takes a deep breath in and prepares to launch.

"Sing it with me, Sissy."

And my childhood wish to sing *American Pie* with my dad is here. The song I could only once bring myself to whisper, with eyes closed, flows out my own poetic voice to blend with my father's.

By the time we reach the chorus, Dad is bouncing up and down on the bench seat of the car, both hands on the wheel. I crank the volume up and the speakers crackle in the station wagon.

The song quiets.

A tear falls from my father's eye. He reaches over, pats the centre of the seat, inviting my hand to his.

He slips his pinky through mine and leans toward me, closing the gap on the wide bench seat.

Singing this will be the day that I die.

And just like that, another piece of code was cracked for how to reach my father.

That summer my father drove down the road in the first real muscle car he ever owned; a 1967 cherry red Pontiac GTO, bought for a hundred bucks he'd squirrelled away from his pay cheques. Danny and I stood on the sidelines of the drive, our fists balled up in excitement as he pulled it into the garage. This was the worn-out car we were going to rebuild from scratch. Armed with a stack of *Tradin' Times* my father found new life, staying out late into the night, this time happy. If I wandered out to keep him company, he put me to work, sticking me behind the steering wheel, "Now, turn the wheel, to the left Sissy, no, no, the other left," while he toiled underneath.

Dad started taking money off the top of his pay, just so he could line his wallet with cash for parts he needed. Mom was furious with the change and compensated by lifting twenties from his trousers while he slept. My father napped just hours a night but when he slept, he was out, complete with his mouth hanging wide open. He called this "catching flies" and demonstrated the look with an audacious snore just to get me to laugh. He kept five pillows at his disposal, one under his head, one between his ankles, another tucked between his knees and two more stuffed between his arms like a pliable body he could punch until just so. By the time he drifted off, he was barricaded tightly into a wall of his own making. His back curved away from Mom and her spot in the bed, she slipped the money into her empty jewellery box and stayed up late with a night-light, turning the pages of a gift catalogue.

Summer weekends were spent combing the dirt paths of junkyards for parts and, on occasion, Danny and I meandered with Dad down the isles of parking lot swap meets, picking up anything that looked like an old car part to run over and see if he wanted to buy it. My father placed ads in the *Tradin' Times* for the odd lots he found along the way and, soon enough, calls started coming to the house. Did he have a radiator for a 1968 Pontiac? Could he get one? What about a dash emblem? Or a set of wheel wells?

When Mom picked up the phone and it was another call for Dad, she usually hung up and let it ring off the hook if they called back. But if I could get it in time, I took messages and slipped Dad the paper when he came home from work. It wasn't just about earning brownie points; each call was contact with the outside world. And in my mind, the voices on the other end belonged to boys my age, boys who might fall in love with me the first time they saw me when they came down the road. I noticed a new-found quality of allure in my voice and heard theirs soften as we bantered back and forth. The thought I might be discovered was exciting and I peeked through the screen of my bedroom, holding out a secret hope that one of them might like me.

But the callers who drove down our dirt road to pick through parts in the garage were not nubile young bucks who wanted to hold my hand at the movies. They were cut of the same cloth as my father and, in addition, fat, old and bald.

Some nights, I got to talk with Dad more than anyone, explaining what the customer had asked for and relaying the conversation verbatim. And before summer was out, my father announced that he had ordered business cards and named our operation after his two beautiful kids; Danny and Julie. And just like that "D&J GTO" bonded the three of us in a way that no shopping spree with Mom or knockdown drag-out fight could ever do. I was smug with pride over our classic car in the making and Dad put me in charge of shipping out parts to customers that lived too far away to come down.

For each car part that was ordered, I fashioned a box with a paring knife and a roll of duct tape, stretching corrugated cardboard over the angular edges of bumpers and fly wheels and stacking hubcaps between piles of newspaper. Little things got wrapped in paper and big things ended up looking like deformed Christmas presents, L-shaped and oblong, thick on one end, skinny at the other. Dad printed up return address labels with our initials in bold blocks and I signed my name underneath in cursive, adding curls on the "J" to make sure customers knew I was a girl. And when the orders added up, the UPS man would fly down our dirt road, sending up a great cloud of dust in the brown van's wake.

I took pride in walking barefoot across the razor sharp gravel we shovelled over the drive each summer; how fast I could toughen up my feet to do it without wincing while carrying a large box of car parts was indication of my strength.

"Hey, Dad," I'd yell to my father in the garage, "Check it out!"

My torso leaned back to counter the weight and I carried the long box of a bumper as carefully as I would a new-born baby while my tender soles felt their way across gravel as sharp as glass.

Knowing car parts, calling out the difference between a '69 and a '79 model of car and playing name that tune to oldies on the car radio with my father at the wheel was the equivalent of winning erasers and biblical lapel pins in Sunday school. I never recalled a single verse memorized on sight, but that was never the point.

At Trader Bud's Roadside Jewelry, Buy-Sell-Trade, I finger a string of pearls on a display rack while Mom heaps fake turquoise jewellery on the counter; blossom necklaces that will hang between her breasts and big gaudy earrings; plastic turquoise teardrops flanked by rhinestones. The pearls are the most delicious shimmery light pink I have ever seen. If I had them, I would be a girl. I would wear them everyday. I would grow my nails and paint them to match. And, even if I was lugging a bumper in an oil-smeared cardboard box out to the UPS man, who sat swivelling in his seat three feet off the ground staring down at me as I struggled with the heavy load in my bathing suit and bare feet, I would still feel like a princess in my pearl necklace.

"Honey, you want those? I'll get them for you, Sissy. Why not? Your mother's robbing me blind."

Later I sat in the back seat of the car, fingering the iridescent plastic beads. I wanted to roll one around in my mouth, to swallow the gift my father had given me; the first present I ever remember him buying for me. I did not know if I had ever been happier in my fourteen years.

That night, in the dark trailer hallway, my father stops me to share the story of how when he was my age, he used to pop his zits with the rim of a Coke bottle heated to glowing by a lighter. He suctioned it to his face while it drew out the spot, than splattered it on all his friends who watched too closely in grossed-out wonderment. He hoots at the memory, the whites of his eyes tinted yellow by the paltry globe of light above. And I laugh right along with him, taking just a tiny step back from the hulk of my father's frame, towering in the dark narrow chute of the hallway.

"That's it, Dan, I'm leaving! You care more about that goddamn car than you care about me! Kids get your shit, we're out of here." Mom shoves items in her purse with fury, slamming through the living room, collecting things to take. "And we ain't never coming back, Dan, you hear me?"

Danny and I trudge down the hall and pull the brown grocery sacks out of our closets. It's hard to know if we will ever actually get in the car with our bags or just stand next to Mom as backup to her threats. We carry them out and wait in the living room. Mom leans in, positioned between us, spitting at my father in his chair. Dad stares rock solid at the television, fingers folded upon his chest.

"Come on, Mom, let's go, he won't change," my brother offers at a time when Dad's radar is lowest for remembering it. Whatever comes of this fight will be far more ingrained in his memory than anything said at the start of it. We are perfect manipulators, my brother and I: if we put up a united front against him, our mother reads it as support and may back down. It's a simple equation we work to our advantage.

I stand at the mouth of the hallway, in case Dad chases her through the trailer. Danny stands at the door, in case he bolts for her throat and she has to run outside. Either way, we are our mother's sentries. She will not stop. Poking. Taunting. Talking. All we can do is block the exits to slow Dad down. And we know that Dad charging is the only thing that will make her stop.

"Come, on, Dannnnnnn," Mom chides, "What cha gonna do about it, huh? What's your little faggot ass going to do, get up and beat me?" She wiggles her hips. "Try to show how maaannn you are by hitting me?"

"I'm warning you, woman."

Mom gloats; finally, response.

Danny and I swap looks.

Our father is on his feet, faster than the speed of light. Our mother's hair in his hands, he pulls her head into his chest and drags her against the hutch.

"Stop fucking with me!" Dad screams. He fingers open the hutch door with his free hand and feels for the gun on the bottom shelf.

"You want this? Is this what you want?" He slams the gun to his chest, curving his hand at the wrist to cock the trigger. "For me to scatter myself all over this goddamn trailer? For the kids to see it?" He shoves it in his mouth, the barrel pokes out his cheek.

For a moment we all freeze and my father locks eyes with me. Silently I plead for the gun to slide from his mouth. As it does, he breaks for the door.

Mom follows close on his heels.

"Mom, please," I beg. "Just leave him alone."

"Oh, no," she hollers after him, "You're not going to run away now, Dan."

She stands in house slippers at the mouth of the garage, hands on her hips.

"Sandy," my father sobs from his place in the back of the garage. "Leave me alone, God, I'm begging you," his voice quivers, "Just leave me alone. I'm at my breaking point."

"You're at your breaking point? What about me? What I want to know is what you're going to do about it. Huh? *Dannn?* What is my good-for-nothing bastard-ass husband going to do?"

My father's head is in his hands.

"I'll tell you what you're going to do, not a goddamn motherfucking thing. You won't do a thing, will you Dan?"

"I'll change." Dad's throat is hoarse.

"No you won't, you'll never change."

My father is silent.

"Did you hear that, Julie? Your father said he's going to change. He isn't going to change, is he?"

I want to slip my father through a trap door and zoom away in the peanut mobile. I want us waving out the window on a Sunday as Mr Hoover chugs up a slow grade. I want my father's trademark chipmunk smile shining down upon me. I want to get in our GTO and race out the drive.

"I will," he says, barely a whisper.

"Well, there is going to be change around here." Mom glowers, "Starting right now. Right this instant. You hear me, Dan?"

"Leave me alone, Sandy, please," Dad cries, squeezing his head between his palms. "Please, just stop talking."

Mom inches in, victorious.

"You're going to sell that motherfucking car, that's what you're going to do, Dan. We need the money, I got bills to pay and kids to feed and you spend more time out here diddling around with that piece of shit than you do with your own family. Isn't that right, Julie? Tell him."

I step into the shadows so she doesn't call on me again.

"You are going to shape up or ship out, Dan. That's all there is to it."

"I'll do anything, Sandy," Dad laments. "Whatever you want, just please, please, leave me alone. I just want peace."

"I told you what you're going to do, Dan."

"I'll sell it, just let me get it done first."

"Fine. Get it done." Mom folds her arms over her chest and turns back toward the trailer. "ASAP. And I mean it."

Alone with my father, I can make out his silhouette sitting at his work bench in the back of the garage.

"Daddy?" I ask softly. "Can I get you anything?"

"Yeah," he drawls out slow and far-away. "Put a bullet in my head will ya?"

My father barrels out the road, brewing in silent rage at the wheel. I scan the radio, desperate.

"I'm trying to find some Beatles for us," I offer.

"Why?" he spits, "I don't want to hear that shit."

I try again. "I wish John Lennon hadn't been killed."

"John Lennon was a fucking hippie. And a moron!" my incensed father says. "He had a dream he was going to get shot, he never should have gone out that day. It's his own damn fault. Should have had a gun on him; blasted that motherfucker away as soon as he saw him."

I stare out the window. Dad's only hero, killed in real life, dead in my father's heart.

"I got my life insurance policy right here." He pats his pocket. "Blow them away before they can blow you away."

Mom adds the *Tradin' Times* to the pile of catalogues she looks through at night. Within a month, she's bought three small-breed show dogs out of the back of the paper: a Pekinese, Yorkshire Terrier and Shit-zu with the perfect lineage, she says, for having litters of puppies. At first we keep them in the trailer and I love folding the cuddly little dogs under the covers with me at night, but after too many accidents in the house, they are stuck out in a pen made of chicken wire attached to the side of the garage.

"I'm an animal lover," Mom says to anyone within earshot in line at the grocery or feed and grain store.

She says it with a knowing grin and a nod towards her purchases and sometimes people will strike up a conversation with her about it. Sometimes they just switch check-out lanes.

I climb in the pen with the dogs after school, to give them love and check their food and water. But the lustrous coats they first came with begin to matt and their eyes take on a desperate misery; where they used to jump at the fence, they sometimes now won't even get out of the doghouse. When we run out of pet food, Mom cleans the fridge out and has me put the remains in their pan, where it rots, drawing flies. I have to dump it in the yard and hose out the maggots on the days they don't touch it.

Dad loads the camper onto the bed of the truck so we can all go with him as he tries to sell the car at a classic car show in Chicago.

"What about the little dogs?" I ask Mom.

"Just put three days' worth of food in the pen, they should be all right."

Dad revs the GTO in the driveway and the engine growls. Sad resignation hangs in the air as I guide him up the ramps of the car trailer, hitched to the truck. This was our car. And we never even got to name it.

"Dan, for crying out loud," Mom says on the way. "You got more junk at home you can fuck around with. You can get another car, later, when we have the money."

But we all know we'll never have the money, because Mom will take it off Dad as soon as he gets it.

On the last day of the car show, a man offers to buy it. He waits outside the camper door for Dad to have a moment to think about it. Dad sits at the dinette, head in hands.

"Sandy, I don't really want to sell it."

"Don't start now with that sentimental shit. It's a car, Dan, and you promised. We need the money."

"I already dropped the price, I got more in it than he wants to give me."

"You sell that goddamn car, Dan." Mom fumes, "Sell it or I'm out of here. I'll take the kids and walk home. I am not going back with you if you don't get rid of that piece of shit."

My father sat on the top bunk and cried when he came back in. Mom climbed down from the camper into the parking lot and slammed the door behind her. Finally alone, I sat at my father's feet and touched my fingers to his skinny calf. I knew how helpless he was. I wanted to give him back all the power he had lost in life. My heart took up his cause, no matter how layered or complicated it was. And he knew I was his best friend even if I could never show him alliance in the presence of Mom. You were either with her or against her, in the totalitarian all-or-nothing mentality that dictated my emotions. To go against Mom, even for a moment, meant a bloody nose in the grocery store and a belting in the car when you least expected it. Mom held a grudge and she never forgot even a wavering of total support for her. And Dad was so low on the totem pole, if I fell from grace by sticking up for him, he would not take a verbal beating for my physical one. This much I understood. It was one more intricate layer I turned a blind eye to.

At the end of the day, we head back home. The car is gone, bought by the man who waited outside our camper to get a good deal on Dad's dream. He gave the GTO to his teenager, the same thing Dad wanted to do with his own kids.

The first thing I remember from my fifteenth birthday was crying. Dad was late. Too late. And, being tuned to my father, I knew when something wasn't right. The panic wasn't so much in not knowing what had happened, but in not being with him to take it on myself. At least then I'd have a hand in the outcome. Dad was like a pet Grizzly I'd had since a cub, soft and cuddly as we rough housed in the early years. But he became a different animal as he grew older and I, as his keeper, was the only one he trusted – and the only one who knew how to handle him. The world backed him into a corner, Mom poked him with a stick and little Danny was still too much of a mama's boy to understand what Dad needed. But I did. And if he wasn't with me, I had no control. If something happened to Dad, it happened to me. And it was all my fault.

Mom carries out the grocery store birthday cake, lit with striped candles.

"Where is that son of a bitch?" She drops it on the table.

"Figures," she says, "He'd forget your fucking birthday. Hell, he forgot our anniversary."

"He probably didn't forget." I fleck at the pale pink polish on my nails. "Maybe he's just late."

"What, are you stupid? It's almost dark, Julie! Your father works first shift, seven to three." Mom clucks, "To hell with it," and lights the candles. "We're having your goddamn birthday now, with or without him."

I sit before the flaming cake and smile at my brother, widening my eyes like Dad does when he's trying to cheer us up in a glum moment. My little brother's chin rests on an outstretched arm across the table. He burrows his face into his elbow, hiding tears.

Wax pools at the base of each candle, rivulets winding out over the icing.

Danny peeps an eye over his arm, "Make a wish first."

Make a wish, make a wish. I wish my father to come home all right. I wish Mom to leave him alone. I wish Danny happy. I wish everything to be okay.

In one long puff, I blow out the candles.

But my father does not come.

Twilight streaks sherbet and peach across the sky, the sun drops beneath the last of the tree line behind the trailer.

When the phone rings, we jump.

"That fucking son of a bitch." Mom slams the receiver down. "He lost his job at Sherex. Some guy is driving him home. The idiot went to the roof with his gun to jump. Jesus, they thought he was going to shoot somebody. They could have put him in jail."

I think of my father perched at the edge of the roof, his square prescription lenses shading dark as the sun glints off that beautiful building. Tapping into his thoughts, I don't feel anger in him standing there, only an immense sense of hopelessness. It is the scenario of the car rocking over him in the drive, all grown up. I imagine getting the call and rushing up to Columbus. I'm the only one they let up on the roof. I'm the only one who can reach him. I inch toward my father while co-workers anxiously wait at the edge of the stairwell. It would be just like the movies, with Dad eternally grateful for me saying just the right words. I'd walk down with him and everyone would cheer and pat him on the back, happy he'd decided to come down. We'd get in the car and drive home. And if Dad was divorced, Mom would never have to know. That would be a great birthday.

A rumble sounds at the top of the road, car tyres rolling into gravel, just not Dad's beater. The car slows at our mailbox and turns into the drive. I run out bare-foot to meet Dad before Mom can get her shoes on. I have never seen him in the passenger seat before. He is always behind the wheel. My father steps out and the car backs into the road, picking up speed as it rounds the first bend.

He stands alone in the gravel. I can barely make out his silhouette, faded against greys and midnight blues of dusk. He holds perfectly still, his grey plastic lunch box still in hand.

"Dad?" I call out, "Dad, where are you? Are you okay?"

Only the smallest "no" lifts from my father and I trace the sound. I hear his lunch pail slip from slack fingers to land in the drive. As I near, my father begins to cry in the dark. I drape his leaden arms around my shoulders and he folds over me like an orangutan, quaking.

"It's okay, Dad, it's going to be okay."

"I lost my job. I don't have anything."

"It's okay, Dad. It's okay."

"I thought if I jumped I'd be worth more dead than alive. Your mother took out a life insurance policy on me. At least you'd have the money then."

"We don't want any money, we just want to be with you. Okay? Okay?"

"It's your birthday today, isn't it?"

"Yeah, but that's okay, I'm just glad you're home."

"I wanted to get you something nice. But I don't have any money." Dad cries on my shoulder.

I cry with him. I can never refuse my father.

The screen door slams and Mom appears as a dusky shadow in the warm May night. She carries a grocery bag full of clothes in her arms, like the ones she makes us keep in our closets.

"Get in the car," she instructs my father.

Dad clings to my hand.

"Dan, get over here and get in the car." Mom paws her foot in the rocks like a crazed stallion. "I am not fucking around with you, now come-onnn!"

She throws the sack of clothes through an open window into the back seat.

"I don't want to go," my father whispers.

"Mom," I shout, "Where are you guys going? Where are you taking Dad?"

"Don't worry about it, I'll talk to you kids later. Dan, get over here."

My heart races as I watch my father walk like a zombie to the car.

He wiggles his fingers out the open car window. "Bye, bye, Sissy."

Then sings it like the saddest song from the *Sergeant Pepper's* album, "*Bye, Bye*."

"Watch your brother," Mom slams behind the wheel. "I'll be back in a few hours."

Danny and I sit on the couch and wonder where Mom is taking him. The local hospital? The police station? To see a doctor? To the dog pound? We ruled out the police station; Mom was terrified of cops. And Dad didn't have a doctor. It was better to think of him going to the hospital, to make sure he wasn't hurt. I imagined him talking to a nice person who he could joke with, while Mom had to wait outside. My father would return that night, and everything would be okay.

But Mom returned alone and this time, she was ecstatic.

"They took him!" she shouted, expecting us to be equal in our joy. "He's in the looney bin. I can't believe it, they locked the bastard up."

My heart sank. I tried to muster a few words but was scrambled by the fear of not having Dad near. Without him, I was lost, just a crippled girl, limping on her one good leg. And without him to hide behind, the world would still laugh at me and kids would be cruel.

Mom clucks her mouth in satisfaction, "I can't believe they locked your father up! God, I hope they throw away the key."

Chapter Five

The Veteran's Administration Hospital is parked on a lonely stretch of broken-down highway that swings wide around the small town of Chillicothe, leading those driving on it far from the main drag. As Chillicothe fades, the Mohekin County maximum correctional facility springs into view, wavering like a mirage through the windshield, its intricate fence system cutting along the highway. Three rows of jagged razor blades loop atop a two-storey heavy-gauge fence that runs alongside the car for miles. Chain-link yards inside the main fence shrink back towards the buildings, hemming the prisoners into smaller and smaller chutes.

The dusty wind kicks through the open windows. My brother cries softly in the back seat, his Matchbox car attaché case beside him. I stare out of the car and watch fields of sweet peas roll by, their tangled leaves suspended off the ground, making a blanket that rolls over hills and valleys for miles.

Mom snaps her gum in smaller and smaller bubbles, lost in a daydream.

"Wouldn't it be great kids – I mean just food for thought – if they kept your father? It would be just the three of us, we could do whatever we wanted. We could go on a cruise down to Florida, go to Disney World while we were there. Wouldn't that be fun? I've always wanted to go to Sea World, see Shammu. We'd get your father's disability cheques and the hospital would take care of him down here."

Mom starts to pack, tallying up which clothes to bring and what shoes go with what wigs. Danny presses his hands between his knees and topples over in the backseat, heaving an audible line of sniffles.

We drive past military memorial plots where a thousand white wooden crosses blur by in geometric design. A skunk lies disembowelled on the side of the road, a host of flies swarming round its open mouth.

Just up ahead a white wooden sign comes into view: Veteran's Administration Hospital, Chillicothe. White stone pillars mark the hospital entrance and between them a single paved lane stretches into the distance. Ancient trees tower over the road, leaning in, their branches tangling in a canopy like the outstretched arms of children playing London Bridge.

Mom slows the car to a crawl. A deserted golf course sprawls to the left and a stately mansion sits deteriorating at its edge, gleaming in the bright summer sun. Its evergreen shutters are a crisp contrast to a once pristine white. An American flag wilts on its pole with barely so much as a ripple, as if it is too hot to even move.

Mom checks a bit of scrap paper sticking out the top of her purse. "We're looking for building number 35."

Danny and I bolt our eyes on signs as they pass, listing the number of each building. The structures all look the same, like four-storey brick apartment buildings set several hundred feet from the lane, but the numbers follow no logical sequence, jumping from building 10 to building 100 through 108, then back to building 20.

We drive past them all and, just as the lane curves sharply to lead again out to the main road, the sign for Dad's building appears. Building 35 is set back from the rest of the compound and tucked behind the sight line of the other structures. The back of the building is naturally fenced by a line of soaring pines, their long feathery branches sweeping low to the ground, heavy and drooping over beds of fallen needles that pile like matchsticks waiting for a light.

The pines run along dense woods that seem to swallow the landscape as far back as the eye can see, neither deterring or inviting escape.

Men shuffle through the parking lots and stand along corridor walls; some are dressed, others don striped pyjama bottoms and a few sit parked in wheelchairs, their chins slumped onto their shoulder, drooling. Cigarette butts lie strewn haphazardly over the sidewalk outside the entrance, some trailing smoke.

Mom opens the heavy double doors and the eyes of idle men fall upon her as she marches us past in her white summer pumps.

After checking in with the visitor desk, she hits the elevator button for the third floor.

"Kids, you don't have to talk to your father if you don't want to. He doesn't need to know what we talked about in the car. That needs to stay just between us. If he asks you if you want him to come home, tell him you want him to stay here."

I squeeze my little brother's hand. We follow Mom down the hall.

The concrete walls are shock white and it looks like a prison. The barred windows have a film over the glass so only muted light filters through. The beautiful pines outside are nowhere to be seen from the third floor of building 35. The door of my father's wing is heavy-gauge steel. A long skinny window runs down the side, a crisscross of wire mesh embedded in the glass. Danny and I stand behind Mom as she presses the buzzer to let the nurse know we're here. The door buzzes unlocked and the nurse tells us which room our father is in.

My heart races to see Dad. It's seemed so long since he's been gone but it's only been a few days. When Mom stops at the room number, Danny and I cross the threshold. Dad slumps on the edge of the bed with his back to the door.

"Dad?" Danny and I sing.

"Kids?" Dad says, his voice sticking as if it hasn't been used since he got here.

My beautiful father sits in an open-back gown, his hair smooshed against his head in a sideways pillow crest. His eyes gloss over as we rush him, wrapping our arms around his body, so much smaller and colder than I can ever remember.

Danny presses against Dad's bare knee and cries. When I see my brother's tears, my own dam breaks, until my bottom lips sucks in and out like a baby. My father hooks his hands around our necks like lobster claws and pulls us close. He nestles his face into my hair and my skin grows moist with his tears. His big palm folds over the smallness of my brother's skull, Danny's summer blond locks poking up through Dad's spread fingers.

Mom stands against the wall, the purse strap folded through arms crossed over her chest. Her white pumps press together and her mouth twists down.

My father pulls back to look me in the eye.

"I love you like crazy, Sissy."

I squeeze my father tight. "I love you too, Dad."

* * *

"Julie, come in here," Mom yells from the bathroom. I squeeze next to her at the basin. My mother places her index fingers on the outside of her eyes. She pulls the skin up on her forehead, stretching her face taut. She gives the mirror a tight smile.

"Don't you think I'd look better with a facelift?"

"You don't need one Mom."

"Well, we'll see what happens at this hearing for your father. It's not like I've got your skin." She slips her bony fingers around my chin, peers in close.

"Come over here in the light."

Mom stands me against the bathroom counter and digs the curve of a bobby pin into my soft cheek. A pimple pops out but the half moon of the metal stays imprinted on my skin.

"We're going on that cruise, Julie," Mom mumbles, holding another bobby pin between her lips. "You are going to help me in this. You hear me?"

She pulls out the blackhead extractor ordered from the *Fingerhut Catalogue* and rakes my face with her fingers, preening me with a vengeance. She is searching for blackheads and by God she will find one. When she does, she pins me to the bathroom counter, pressing against me. She suctions the tip of the blackhead extractor to what she is sure is a menacing spot. Her face inches from mine; I hold my breath, sucking in and out from the corner of my mouth like breathing with a reed under water; anything to not let her breath touch mine.

Mom's plan is a brick wall in her mind and I can't find a way to scale it. The more she talks of Disney and the cruise, the more she believes it's just weeks away – if they just will just keep my father. The more she wants them to keep him, the more she demands total alliance from me. The sands beneath my feet are shifting; where once I could only think of protecting Dad from her, now I can only think of saving myself.

Mom adds up what she could probably get for him as the fiduciary for his disability cheques, then what pension he might have when she cashes it in with the government. She makes a list of all the money she could collect, from selling off Dad's garage piece by piece to how much the life insurance policy will be. Then duplicates her list on every piece of scrap paper in the house.

"We'll have to make some small changes in our lifestyle," she says, "but basically we'll get to stay here and finally enjoy life for once." All things are possible without my father. She confides in me and I nod as I always do, with secret panic at how to walk the fine line keeping her happy and getting Dad home.

The weeks slip past and Mom stops taking us to see Dad. As each day rolls by, my heart aches more for my him but the tripwires I have become used to living with strung all around us have gone slack. I can hear the birds in the trees outside and wander around in the woods, making hooting calls to see who will answer back.

I miss my father. But I also feel guilty for the growing sense of relief that he's not here. Do I miss Dad, or the feeling of control that came from looking out for us? Out in the world, everything Dad did was reckless, infused with potential threat that soaked my brain with adrenaline. And without it, I started to withdraw, feeling as if something was terribly wrong. And a month later, a thought comes into my head: maybe what was wrong was Dad's reaction to the world all along.

Mom slams the phone down.

"Jesus Christ," she hisses, "Your father tried to escape. He punched his fist through the security window. The moron severed the artery in his hand, nearly bled to death on the floor before they got to him. Get your shoes on, kids, I've got to go down there and sign some shit." Mom slips into her duck boots, with the backs mashed down.

Danny and I race around grabbing anything we think Dad might like to have.

My father paces like a tiger down the hall, his hands clasped behind his back, the gown flowing behind him as freely as church robes.

Dad's hand and wrist are wrapped in white gauze and look like the giant tip of a matchstick.

"Hey, Sissy!" he shouts out.

Danny and I run to him. I touch the bandage.

"Yeah, I cut myself."

"I'm sorry," I whisper.

"I missed you guys." He looks down at us. "So I tried to come home."

My father's eyes flash panic.

He lowers his voice. "I've got to get out of here, Sissy."

"I know, Dad, I know."

"I'm going crazy in here."

Danny stands at Dad's knee, "I want you to come home too, Dad."

"We miss you so much. I want you to come home."

"You don't get it do you?" Dad's good hand grips me like a hawk, "You have to help me get out of here." His

111

eyes widen in terror, "Please, please help me." His thumb rubs my hand furiously until it Indian burns, "You have to help me, Sissy, you're the only friend I got."

I've cried so many times with my father; his hand hooked over the back of the car seat clinging to mine, misty eyes in the rear-view mirror, him on milk crates in the garage, face buried in his hands, as I patted his back and cried in frustration for him, spooning poached eggs on toast as his arms clung to his chest.

But this time it's different.

I can't stop Mom and I can't spring him out. I don't know what to do; except stay in the separate tracks of both parents as I've always done, buying some time until I can figure it out. Mom doesn't know I want Dad home and if we let on and go against her plans, she will kill me. Dad has no idea how convincing I have to be with Mom. I have to get him out; I'm the only one he's got. But it's Mom I have to live with.

Mom walks over. "Kids, say goodbye, the nurse has to give your father his meds."

I squeeze my father's hand.

"No, Sissy, don't go. They give me pills that put me to sleep." My father's eye cloud with panic. "They're going to kill me. They're going to kill me in here. One of these days, I won't wake up." He grips my hand. "Please don't leave me."

"Dan," Mom spits, "Just cut it out."

"Kids," she snaps her fingers, "Get over here. *Now*."

I peel my hand from my father's, sweat and tears mixed together on my skin. My mind races, the floodgates drawn with everything running for its life.

We walk away and the nurse slips in his room.

Think, think. I have to do something.

I can hear my father shouting, "Help me Sissy, don't let them do this!" all the way down the hall.

Mom gets down on her hands and knees right there on the screened-in Astroturf porch of a complete stranger's house and jacks off their male Pekinese with her own bare hand, squeezing his stuff into an empty Cool Whip tub she fishes from her purse. She pulls out the turkey baster and sucks it up with the mustard-coloured bulb. It's the same one she bastes the Thanksgiving turkey with.

"Julie, for Christ's sake, will you help me over here, you can see I'm struggling."

I can barely bring myself to move.

"Hold the dog," she says.

Mom checks her with dirty fingers.

"Godammit, Julie, hold her still, I gotta see if she's ready."

I tense my arms so it only looks as if I'm holding tighter. I lock my arms out straight and pivot my head to look out the screen door.

In the yard next door there's a girl my age jumping on a big, round trampoline. Her long blond hair bounces in the summer sun. *I used to have hair like that.* I see us with our long blonde locks, holding hands, bouncing up and down and laughing like best friends. Our mothers are in the kitchen setting the table for Sunday pot roast and our fathers yell out the back, *Girls, dinner's almost ready.* They trot through the yard and scoop us off the trampoline into solid arms. Dad throws me over his shoulder, strong and gentle. The other Dad shouts, *Tickle Attack!* and our ribs implode with shockwaves from digging fingers. We kick our tanned legs wildly and shriek in mock horror. The dog slips from my hands and darts to a corner of the porch.

"For Christ's sake, I'll fucking do it myself. Go sit in the car."

She pushes me out of her way and stomps past. I turn my back on the girl and look through the window of the porch to the golden glow of the living room where the stud owners sit. They are watching *PM Magazine* from the safety of matching plaid recliners. They've retrieved their stud dog and he is in the kitchen now, bouncing up wildly on his hind legs behind the baby gate, his silky Pekinese tail pure sheen from daily brushing. The owners casually drink from cans of Faygo perched on neat cork coasters. They do not care about the little dog huddled in the corner of their Astroturf enclave, with her matted underbelly and the nest of flea eggs clustered in her coat. She is only eight months old. They will choose the pick of the litter in turn for the stud fee and if that doesn't pan out, they'll at least get 200 dollars for my mother's hand job on their boy.

Mom looms over the female, grabs her scruff and carries her out of sight of the owners in case they turn to look out the screen door.

She pins her neck to the floor, "Now hold still you little bitch."

With her other hand, she snakes the tube into the female, plunges the syringe.

The dog thrashes, Mom yanks her tail up.

I could have died.

"God. I hope she catches." The dog's back legs dangle in mid air, helpless.

I am nothing like this person I call "mother".

I'm only like the little dog, the one she calls "bitch", same as me.

"Take this one, I don't think it's going to make it." I cradle the puppy's body, soft as salmon bones. Lifeless and warm, I tuck it behind my back as Mom pulls another one out.

She is so anxious to see how many puppies she will get, less the one going to the stud owners, that she is "helping" with the delivery.

She threw the last puppy that died right over the baby gate, and the slick stillborn landed in the kitchen trash can like a crumpled-up piece of paper.

"Slam dunk," she said.

This one I slip behind my back. I will sneak it out in a paper bag as one of my most cherished possessions and bury it under the knarled roots of the old apple tree.

The puppies barely have their eyes open, their soft paper nails fail as they try to climb the sides of the box on the other side of the baby gate. The mother jumps frantically at the gate and barks. The puppies slide down the side of the box again and again, whimpering.

I hate it.

I could swear that the dark stain that runs from the inside of the Pekinese's eyes down her face is the stain of her tears. I kneel on the ammonia-soaked papers of the laundry room and hold her tight. She struggles, she only wants her babies. I cry with her, *I'm so sorry, I know, I know*.

In the car on the way to the pet store, I lean against the window.

Mom chides, "Anyone that's going to pay five hundred dollars for a goddamn dog is going to give it a good home, Julie."

You do.

The puppies yip in the back seat.

"For Christ's sake stop sulking, I do and do and do for you kids and what the fuck, I can't even make a little money for my own goddamn self around here. Jesus Christ."

She pulls behind Petland to the delivery door.

"Wait here." She grabs the box from the back seat. The puppies go sliding and land in a huddle in the lower corner.

"If they come out and ask you how old these babies are, you tell them eight weeks, got it?"

Back in the car, she pulls a wad of cash from her purse and counts it. She was counting it before we even got here. She's been counting it in her head over and over for the last five weeks.

I stare out the window as Mom drives us to the hospital. We are attending a hearing held by Dad's doctors to see if he should stay at the hospital as a patient and collect disability or if he should be sent back home. Mom coaches me what to say in the car.

"It's down to you, Julie. And you need to do the right thing for your father."

Tears slip from my eyes and I can't bring myself to look at her.

She reaches over and squeezes my knee to the bone. I can't go against Mom. I can't go against Dad.

"You're going to tell him that he beats me, that he carries a gun. Tell them you're scared of him."

I'm terrified to say anything.

"Listen, it's not like your Dad's going to be there, watching you. This is just a preliminary hearing, it's the family and his doctors. You can tell them anything, it's confidential; it's not going to get back to your Dad."

* * *

There are more people in the hearing room than Mom said there would be, a whole table of men with notebooks and papers scattered before them. They look official.

When it's my turn, I feel faint. I sit in the chair on the raised platform, the room is dead silent.

"Miss Gregory, it has been requested by your mother that you share with those at the hearing today what your feelings are about your father."

I nod.

"Are you scared of your father, Miss Gregory?"

I don't think so. I'm not scared when he's crying. But I don't exactly know. As long as I'm with Dad, I can fine-tune things. It's when I'm not that I'm terrified.

"No," I say.

Mom fixes me in an effervescent glow of control. It surrounds my chair like a bubble. I can see her out of the corner of my eye. *We talked about this in the car. We rehearsed what questions they were going to ask. I told you what to say. Don't sit there like a bump on a log.*

"Do you want your father to come home?"

"Yes," and Dad's side takes the lead. I do want Dad to come home. I just don't know when.

Mom clears her throat, "Excuse me, Julie was just telling me in the car on the way here that Dan has hurt her and she's scared of him. Weren't you, Julie?" she glowers.

"Yes." And Mom scores the point.

"Has your father ever hit you?" they ask.

I stare at my knees and trace a design on my skin.

Danny is only a baby the first time Dad turns on me. My baby brother lies sleeping in his carrycot as Mom runs down the list of instructions for the babysitter. My father stands by the door, staring at me. Mom finishes with the sitter and Dad turns to her. He yanks his belt from his pants, makes a loop and cracks it in the air.

I flinch. The sitter stands frozen.

"See this?" He glares at me, only seven, then looks to her. "Don't be afraid to beat the living shit out of her if she gets out of line."

The man who said that is not the Dad who scoops me up at the door and plays This Little Piggy went to Market with my toes. This was the first time I saw Dad with dark clouds rolling behind his eyes and a voice that had already hit me. And it split me like a tree cracked by lighting.

My arms hang leaden in the chair; I wiggle my fingers to check them.

Mom clears her throat. I can see her mouthing *yes,* her lips wide and exaggerated. She raps her one unbroken press-on nail on the seat of her wooden chair, waiting.

"Has he hit you before?"

"Yes." My voice is not my own.

"What else has he done to you?"

Nothing. My father has never touched me. Don't even think that.

And I'm fetching for Dad on a summer afternoon. Mom is on the warpath and Dad is sunk in his chair. He has me run to make him a diet pop. He likes it just so, in a big plastic tumbler full of ice. But I'm taking too long in the kitchen and Mom is baiting him. It's the third dynamic between us: Mom whips Dad into a frenzy and slowly clips away at the thin veneer of trust between us all.

"Are you just going to let her make fun of you like that, Dan? You don't get any respect from that girl, she's in there dilly-in around. You asked her five minutes ago to get you something to drink. I'm standing right here, I can see her in there flipping you off behind your back. Are you just going to sit there and take that?"

And Dad is up out of his chair, storming the kitchen. He grabs the tumbler off the counter and flings it at me. Soda and ice hit my face as he knocks me back into the corner of the kitchen, his fists take me down. Grabbing the countertop as leverage, he hauls his boot back to kick me in the stomach. I curl like a garden grub and turn black and blue.

"Do you want your father to stay here in the hospital?" the men ask.

Mom taps a few times on the seat, Morse code that this is it. Do it now or get it in the car. She covers with a cough.

"Yes." It's the other voice, speaking through me.

I can feel her sigh relief. I have told them what she wanted. It's her I have to live with, not Dad. It's done. For the first time since they put me up here, I lift my eyes from my knees.

A dozen people are scattered around the hearing room, but one pair of eyes in ghostly grey burn a hole right through me. The eyes of my father.

Mom told me he wouldn't be here. She told me he'd never know what I said.

My father sits in the last row, staring through me stone cold. Even with a full shaggy beard, I can see his jaw clamped tight. I beg him with my eyes; *she made me do it.*

He shrugs. And I know it doesn't matter. She may have chosen the words, but they came out of my mouth.

Chapter Six

The results of the hearing reached us in October. I was still fifteen but felt so much older. The verdict was in: Dad was coming home. Despite the damning testimony by both Mom and I on the stand, his doctors had decided he was perfectly capable of managing out of the hospital. The entire five months my father had been gone, Danny and I had never talked once about what might have landed Dad on a locked ward to begin with. To us, the event seemed like just another injustice Dad had suffered in the normal plight of marriage. Dad might have driven the car, but Mom had her foot on the gas and the brake.

In response to the news, Mom stomped through the trailer thinking up ways to appeal the decision so she could still get the money. She made endless phone calls to the hospital in Chillicothe, trying to track down the specific people who decided to spit Dad back.

But it didn't matter what the doctors thought. It only mattered what Dad did. And within a few short days he was going to be home. Whenever I tripped upon the memory of what I'd said at the hearing and how my father watched me without my knowing it, I shut my eyes fast and shook my head in panic. But I couldn't forget. And neither would Dad. It would be one of those things we would take to the grave unresolved. But I knew if I could just make it up to my father, I could win back his love as I had before.

From the moment Dad walked through the door that October, we never said a word about where he'd been. The gap closed with fresh stitches when he hugged us both, perfectly happy to be home. I tiptoed through the fall on eggshells, constantly popping my head in the living room to check his mood. But the infinite small details of what went down that summer were swept away. The only outward sign of anything amiss was the gully carved in the crook of his hand and the bright red slash that ran through it. And when Mom's carefully hatched plan for a lifetime of collecting on Dad turned to dust, she embraced him with a newfound niceness to have him back as the breadwinner.

But something had changed in my father; where the days leading to his hospitalization ticked with velocity. Those following his release felt as if all the air had been let out of them in a slow leak. A haze fogged my father like mists of cloud on a mountain peak and his body, tipped as always at ninety degrees in his chair, was as lifeless as if he'd been wrapped in carpet and spritzed with a garden hose.

For the first time in my life, I saw my father take pills. Prescription drugs from little vials on his bedside. There were pills to take when he woke, pills to take at night and others for in between. Through the days and nights, my father dozed by the soft glow and white hush of the television. He could not wake up.

But the biggest difference came in the quiet moments in our now calm trailer. Gone was the booming larger-than-life presence of my father when he was pounding down the hall or cackling in boisterous glee or letting out a belch that would carry to the back of the trailer. The TV stayed at an ear-straining minimum volume and, when he walked from the front to the back of the trailer down the hall, I had to peek out my bedroom door to even know it was him. Our trailer fell eerily quiet, not with the calm before the storm but from the lack of storm altogether.

And when I said, "Hi, Dad," as I did twenty times a day to check he wasn't brewing angry at me he simply said, "Hi, Sis" each time right back.

I'd offer, "Dad, can I get you anything?" hoping he would have me fetch him something that would earn me a timed response and a shout of praise but my father, reclining with his hands tucked between his legs, would think for a moment and say, "No, thanks, I'm all right."

Something was definitely wrong with him.

The only way Dad could apply for disability was to make a plea for it before a court in Washington DC. He also wanted to visit The Wall, the newly built historical monument holding the names of fallen soldiers. There were three friends he had lost in Vietnam, he told me, and he wanted to pencil shade their names on tracing paper. That way he could keep them close forever. Dad grew misty eyed and asked if I would come with him. I didn't miss a beat in saying yes. This would be our first road trip ever and a chance to spend a few complete days with my father; something I hadn't done since I was his baby.

We headed out on the highway in the truck and camper, my father mellow at the wheel. I cannot remember such peace with him in a car since he loaded up cantaloupes and drove me to the base to sell them.

Dad drives straight through the day. As the night darkens the cab of the truck, I think about where we're going to sleep. The camper is on the back but I don't want to sleep in such close quarters. The thought of being next to Dad belching, farting and scratching through the night fills me with dread. Besides, he has promised he'll get us a hotel room with double beds at least the first night.

We arrive in the city close to midnight, the deserted streets wet with cold rain. I worry that Dad will back out of his promise if I don't press him for where we're going to stay.

"Well, if you can find us a room for under eighty dollars, Sis, I'll do it. Otherwise, we're just going to have to stay in the camper. We can find a parking lot that's lighted; it'll be just like a hotel."

He pulls up next to a ritzy place and has me run in. I know even getting out of the cab of the truck that this hotel is expensive. The price is way over eighty dollars and I wonder if Dad is really pulling up to places he already knows are going to be too much. He has me run in to two more, each the same. I stand at the counter in crumpled clothes, exhausted from the twelve-hour drive and ask how much a room is. The suited clerk tells me two hundred and twenty-five dollars. I trudge back to the truck and tell Dad.

"Did you ask if they give a Triple A automobile discount?" he laughs.

On our crisp fall walk to visit The Wall, we pass POW-MIA supporters camping out in tents, some chained to protest signs. The structure, completed two years earlier, is a smooth black ribbon of marble that snakes across fields that join some of Washington's most weathered monuments. At the time, over 58,000 names of soldiers were carved in its face. The air all around is sombre and, getting closer, I can feel the heft and weight of the names etched overhead. I remembered the way death felt driving along the long, dusty lane to the slaughter pens as a child and could not help the spring that runs down my face.

My father searched for the names of his friends and I followed behind, knowing he would not keep track of me. Visitors were placing fingers on the etchings and crying, some were slumped at the wall's base as if the mere sight of a loved one's name carried the weight of an entire funeral.

My father found the first one and placed tracing paper over his buddy's name. As he shaded the pencil over the paper and the name emerged, my father began to sob. I stood next to him and cried too. We clung to each other at The Wall, irrevocable sadness surrounding us. I looked around, so many strangers' tears – the one-legged man in camouflage, the dishevelled homeless Veteran, mothers and wives in comfortable shoes, silently mourning.

After finding the other names, Dad leaned his head against the cool granite. He held the paper with the names of his three buddies from high school, the friends he lost in the war, close to his chest.

"They were the best friends a guy could ever have," Dad cries. He wrings his forehead in the palm of his hand and breaks down. "And I signed every one of them up for three extra weeks of leave."

That December Dad takes me to my first rock concert. By now the vials of pills no longer sit on his nightstand and Dad as I know him is making a comeback. He sits at the concert theatre and chows from a giant bag of red pistachio nuts he snuck in. As each nut is plucked from its shell, he spits the carcass directly at the back of a kid's head. Some don't notice, but many run their fingers through their hair, trying to pick out what's hit them. My father keeps a straight face when they turn to find where the flying shell came from; then laughs hysterically when they pivot back around.

"Hey, Sissy, your old man's cool. Watch this." He hawks another shell at the same kid three rows up. It slaps against his face. I think about the kids on the bus who throw crabapples at the back of my head.

"I'm the original wild man!" Dad roars into the sound of the band. I smile at my dad at the same time as I take a step away from him, irritated. The lure of my childhood to win his praise is losing lustre. Being with Dad is like babysitting a little kid or wrangling a full-grown grizzly – and I'm getting just as annoyed with both.

I do not have a single picture of my father and me together. The most we have of us in the same frame are those that illustrate in miserable detail the vacation we took the summer after he came home. We drove cross-country, all four of us, stuffed into the truck camper with Mom packing every nook and cubby with as many pairs of shoes and matching wigs as she could cram into the cabinets and under the dinette.

From the very first picture taken when we hit the Rockies of Colorado, my father tries to stand tall as the pillar of the family. He is wearing his straight-up red-and-blue striped tube socks, an outfit packed for the trip and then picked out for him that morning by Mom while she burnt pancakes in the K-Mart parking lot where we had spent the night. Danny and I flank our father, looking like good kids, playing our part. Mom wears a ridiculous perm that gives her an airy black halo of Afro hair and we smile because that's what we do. We smile in all the Polaroids whether we are terrified, angry or exhausted. We are cornered into those smiles like a wildcat with a chair, bound to them by an echo of consequence that registers somewhere deep inside the folds of our brain what will be set into motion if we don't. Smiling is the lesser of two evils.

As we press westward and the temperature heats up, so does my father's meltdown and the family vacation starts to unravel. Mom and Dad fight from Missouri on and, even when I ride in the camper above, splayed on the master bed to look out the wide window that hangs over the truck cab, I can hear them screaming crystal clear as my father speeds on the highway. Once in Colorado, we cluster in front of the Adolf Coors Brewing Company; my father stands in his flip-flops, his foot and ankle-bone white up to his sock line, the rest of his leg ruddy tan. We all squint into the sun, pressing our hands to our foreheads as visors. And there is one of him alone, positioned before the Painted Desert, with his chipmunk smile, dropping his top teeth over his bottom, looking fragile with his hands stuffed in his pants' pockets, as if willing someone to tip him back over the cliff. As the trip grinds on, my father wears down frame by frame until the last haunting photograph: me perched on a stone wall atop the Colorado River in a jean jacket, my long colt legs stretched out before me, with the kind of flawless hair only achieved through an hour of curl ironing – a feat I came to master in the plastic bathroom mirrors of rest stops along the way, just to get away from my parents. My father sits next to me, a Leonard Cohen sadness in his eyes, sinking himself with rumination and regret: *his GTO gone, his record collection gone, his job gone, his friends gone, his baby gone, his hope gone.*

My sweet brother leans forward into the camera, already with a big-man-on-campus smile thrust out at the lens. He stands at the edge of my mother's cocked knee like a little boy, but his face strives to be the man. As my father is beaten back by Mom, Danny is coaxed into place.

Back home, my father nestles into his chair, his hands fold under his chin like the delicate wings of a morning dove. I peek around the corner from the kitchen, finally finishing the dishes. I will try to sneak down the hall to my bedroom, and pray he doesn't hear me.

"Sis? That you?"

Too late.

"Yeah, Dad."

"I got some peanut brittle I want you to run and get for me."

"Uh, alright." I walk into the living room.

"Here, put my shoes on. It's out in the garage, on my workbench."

"Dad, I'm scared of the dark."

"Pleeease? Do it for me. I'll give you some."

I can never refuse my father.

I slip my bare feet into his work boots.

"You better take the flashlight, I left the light on in the garage and the lights burnt out."

The county night swallows every bit of light you can ever shine into it. There are no lamp-posts, no car headlights, no lit-up sky from the glow of a distant city. I creep in my flannel nightgown and my father's mammoth work boots down the gravel walkway, dragging the laces behind me. The trailer glints in the moonlight as the garage looms ahead against the dark sky. I stand at its mouth with the flashlight, barely making a dent in the heavy shroud.

I inch through, hand held out, bumping into loaded milk crates and tools dumped on the floor. The middle of the garage is scariest, too far into the dark to see anything, too far from the only exit to scurry back. I jimmie the light side to side, widening its path. I press in, heart racing.

I can make out the dark edge of the workbench just ahead. When I touch its corner, I raise the shine of the light from the floor in front of me up over the junk piled beneath it; rolls of colour-coated wire, cardboard boxes smeared with grease, frazzled bits of rusting steel wool, slabs of shingles, alien car parts and various grades of sandpaper.

The light catches on a flash of skin. I peer in close.

It's a knee, a girl's knee, pressed on a page between two cardboard boxes.

I pull out the picture. It isn't just one naked knee, but a tangle of body parts, a girl on a magazine cover, men pressed to her face.

My stomach drops.

In the garage, I grow lost in a stack of naked girls; naked girls whose bent limbs stick out from under heaps of bodies and moustached men who sneer down upon their faces.

Digging deeper with the flashlight, I'm transfixed in the fluorescent world of the grotesque; grimy edged copies of *Ohio Swinger;* where toothless women with rolling fat guts offer dirty talk and their phone number, complete with our own local area code. In my father's garage, by a circle of light, I trip upon an underworld that turns my stomach.

An underworld I cannot bring myself to look away from.

In the living room of our trailer, my antennae tune to the first hint of any television commercial for a feminine product. The moment I hear flowery music or a woman's soft voice, I am off the couch, dashing down the hall to do something of grave importance I forgot to do in my bedroom.

I cannot be a girl like the girls in the garage; I will never let a man with a moustache do those things to me. I will never be what the men in the magazines are waiting for girls like me to be: a bleeder.

Each time I am sent to the garage – to turn out the light, to find Dad's keys, to fetch another case of Tab – the girls call to me from under the workbench. I study their faces, witness to their capture, butterflies catch fire in my stomach and flutter to ash, the words of so many men in the caption of their photographs smeared upon my skin.

Every month I steal from my mother's supply in the wig cabinet and wrap the used pad to the point of mummification in tissue. I carefully remove the trash from the bin, find an empty toilet paper roll, stuff the bundle in it then put it all in an empty box of Irish Spring. If there isn't an empty soap box in the trash, I make one by taking out a new bar and dropping the old one under the hot tap until it dissolves to a sliver.

I lay my burden on the bottom of the trash can, then carefully pile the garbage back in. Nobody's going to catch me with my pants down.

* * *

My sweet sixteenth birthday is just a week away and Dad promises, *promises*, if I'm good, he'll let me go out on my first date. The boy I'm thinking about is from the skating rink. When I can get away from holding Mom's hand, we play Pac-Man and foosball, his shoots and dangs as sincere as his good Christian mouth. Jeff is tall and skinny and the only boy at the skating rink who doesn't look at the girls' butts as they skate past. He goes to school one county over and, outside of the Saturday nights Mom only sometimes skates now, I don't see him at all. I'm giddy at the thought of going out with him.

Driving back from town, my father slows down at a wooded pull-off near our road.

"Boys like to neck," he drawls matter-of-factly.

I cringe.

"And I'd rather know you're safe in one of these spots I'm going to show you than parked behind some building where I don't know where you are." He drives again and as we exit the tunnel of trees that mark the hill descending down into Burns Road, he stops at another unused drive about a mile from home by the marshy bog where the bullfrogs bellow.

"It only takes one carload of niggers to see you behind a building in town, you know, kissing some boy, not paying attention and bam! They shatter the window with a crowbar, rape you, shoot him, throw you in the backseat of their car and I never see you again."

I cannot shake the vision. I don't want to know the men in my father's world, the ones that occupy his mind. I only want to hold hands with Jeff, with a boy who likes me, who could never be like the men in my father's dark thoughts.

Dad faces me. "Listen, boys just want one thing, honey: to put their thing in your thing." I focus on the weeds whizzing past.

"And you're naïve." He explains, "You've been protected your whole life. You don't know boys like I know boys. There are men out there who will slit your throat and leave you for dead. You have to trust me on this. I'm watching out for you."

I know there are boys out there that are different. I know there are boys that my father doesn't know anything about. I don't want him pairing me with the sickos in his mind. I chip the polish of my thumbnail as fast as I can and make a pact with myself: if I can fleck it all off by the time he's done talking, God will make it so that Dad's men will never even look at me.

Mom takes me to Planned Parenthood for her own sex talk.

"When a guy takes you out to dinner, you need to take care of things at the end of the night. He spends money on you and he expects something in return. Your father is letting you go out on dates this summer and the last thing I want is you turning into some kind of baby maker."

I hang my head in the waiting room next to her.

"They'll put you on the pill so that ain't ever going to happen. You take one everyday and don't miss a one."

She flips through a catalogue. "I already raised two kids." Then she pulls another one out of her purse. "Do you think I want to be raising your illegitimate child?"

The night of my first date in late May I stand in the living room while my father gives a last-minute lecture on the midnight curfew from his recline in the La-Z-Boy.

I run to the drive, eager for four hours of freedom. Jeff is nervous; he wipes his sweaty hand down the leg of his jeans but I don't care, I'm free! Every mile Jeff drives us away from Burns Road, I feel less nagged by a worry that Dad has followed me.

At the movies, my arm brushes against Jeff's. I move my hand from the armrest to the seat and feel his hand inch close to mine. Every fibre in my being tunes to the exact location of his every minute movement. I feel his finger reach out, he delicately loops his pinky through mine. I stop holding my breath and curve my pinky around his to hold him to me.

After the movie, we make our way back to Burns Road. There's still an hour before curfew and, with a tinge of embarrassment, I point to the lower drive on the road which Dad drove past only weeks before.

Jeff backs into the spot, cuts the engine and the sound of summer crickets start up, their scratchy legs rubbing in brilliant orchestration. A bat swoops in front of the parking lights, picking off moths that warble toward the glow. We sit in the dark and the quiet folds in around us.

I can hardly find my voice in my throat. Jeff quietly asks me about school and if I want to go to college. We talk about things that barely sixteen-year-olds talk about; feeling humiliated in school, who's popular in our class, who's scummy. Jeff tells me that sometimes the other boys tease him about wanting to wait until he's married but he says he doesn't care. His parents waited and they're still married. He asks if I might want to go to church with him sometime and I can't think of anything better than to hold pinkies with Jeff and sing from the hymnal.

I scoot a little closer and lean my head on his shoulder.

His fingertips trace the tips of my hair. I feel so safe sitting by his side that I almost forget how I came to learn about the enclave where we sit. The conversation of that day flashes through my mind. I shake my head to erase the memory. My father lives in another world. A world I never want to even think about.

Jeff opens his palm to me, a gesture I make out by the faint moonlight through the windshield. I spread my fingers over his and they entwine slow and steady in the most natural feeling in the world. Our hands were made to fit together. He leans his head against my own on his shoulder and I sit with the crickets and the bats, eyes closed, listening to him breathe.

Headlights slam in through the windshield.

I open my eyes to blinding lights. Jeff is yanked from my side as a man's arm shoots through the open window and grabs him, pulling Jeff against the driver's door. He doesn't make a sound. My eyes focus and Jeff's profile is illuminated, staring straight ahead over the steering wheel. In the shadow beside the car lurks my father, one claw pinching Jeff's shoulder, the other with his gun pressed against the cheek of my date.

"Dad! Dad! Dad! We were just talking!"

In a sudden lunge, my father is on the passenger side. He reaches in the open window and grabs my hair.

"You little bitch!" he roars.

My eyes draw to slits as he pulls me over the seat towards the door. My hair clutches in my father's fist like a cave girl, his arms tugging me out the open window as my body torques. He flicks the door handle and I spill to the ground. He collects me by the hair again and drags me across our dirt road, opening the truck door with his other hand and throwing me in like a sack of potatoes. My father storms around the back of the pick-up truck to the driver's side and I steal the seconds to look for Jeff. I cannot see him, only a deserted car flooded in light with both doors flung open.

My father lunges behind the wheel and I brace against the door, clutching the armrest. I hold perfectly still as the seconds tick by. Maybe I can explain. Maybe he will calm down. Is it really past midnight? I thought it was only 11:30 when Jeff last checked his watch.

My fingers stand guard at the door handle, in case my father stops the truck. I imagine flinging the door open as he rolls to a stop, before he can hit me. I wonder how many days I'll have to hide in the woods before I can come home. My father clutches the steering wheel and roars back down the road towards the trailer. There will be about sixty seconds before he has to slow down to turn into our driveway.

I count them.

Sixty. Fifty-nine. Fifty-eight.

If we can just get home before he explodes, maybe I can explain.

"I'm disappointed in you." My father steadies himself through clenched teeth.

Forty-seven, Forty-six.

"I know, I."

He reaches out and I flinch. But instead of hitting me, his fingers wiggle behind my skull to cradle it. The tips grip the bone like so many fingers of a tree frog. I think of my brother's head cradled in my father's big palm in the hospital.

BAM! My face slams into the dash of the truck.

"I'm sorry," I sob.

Thirty-five. Thirty-four.

"I'm sorry."

"Is that all you're going to do? Sit there and smirk? What do you have to say for yourself?"

"Dad. I thought I was doing what …"

Twenty-two. Twenty-one.

My father explodes, "You fucking slut!" His fist strikes my head, knocking me into the passenger window. My head snaps like a doll, my arms useless in my envisioned escape.

"I trusted you!" he screams. I know it can't be heard for a country mile.

He spiders his fingers across the back of my head again, I brace against the dash with weakened wrists.

I pivot at the last second and my brow strikes the cross-bar of the window, pain shoots over my eye. In the dark, I'm as easy to punch as a pillow.

"I'm sorry, Dad," I sob through snot.

Fifteen. Fourteen.

"I'm going to fucking kill you."

"I tried to do what you told me."

"You fucking slut."

Ten. Nine. Eight. Seven.

We pull into the drive, he slams the gearshift into park and rages into the house. I follow close behind.

I know he is blameless. He had to go out in the middle of the night to get me because he was worried sick. Worried I'd been dragged out of the car by a pack of black men, worried I'd been beaten and stolen away from my date.

My father storms down the hall to his bedroom. He tries to slam the door for effect but the cheap press-board only sticks on the carpet, making him furious. He kicks it closed from the inside and screams for his big toe, damning the day of my birth.

I lie in the dark. I can't think straight. I don't know what happened. I try to think back to Jeff, how it felt to have his hand on mine. I know I will never see him again. Tears run down my face, soaking the pillow-case.

The clock in the living room strikes the hour and I silently count the cuckoos – all the way to twelve.

In the morning, my father catches me in the hallway.

"I got an eye on you girl. Get used to it; you ain't going nowhere for the whole fucking summer."

He waggles his finger at me, "You wait right there, I'm going to show you something." My father storms out the front door and appears outside of my skinny bedroom window. I can see his face through the crank-out slats and tiny black grids of the mesh screen.

"Yeah, see that?" He points to a tear in the lower corner of the screen, where the piping that holds it into the frame has lifted from the track. "I know what you've been up to."

He leans in to study it in detail.

"You think you can pull a fast one on your old man? I'm no dummy."

My heart races.

"I've been calculating how long you've been sneaking out. I got it all figured out, you sneaking out this window after I fall asleep and making your way up to the top of the road. Then you wait for a carload of niggers to pick you up, don't you? They pimp you out at Broad and High and drop you back off before I wake up at dawn."

He stops to let this sink in, how clever he's been to catch me red-handed.

"Yeah, I knew it! That's why you had that 'Leave it to Beaver' T-shirt." He unpacks the scenario, detective style. "Even after I told you to throw that thing away, you were sending out Morse code, right under my goddamn nose. You think I'm so stupid, don't you?" he seethes. "That's why you put me in the hospital, isn't it? So you could do your thing without me knowing it."

My mind reels.

"Well, no little slut is going to chump me. You and me," my father pokes the screen. "We're going to tango. I'm going to make your life hell until you come clean and confess or until one of us ends up dead – and it ain't going to be me, got it?"

I can feel my mind warp around my father's logic. Everything can be bent to fit his reality. His thoughts finger into my head until lines blur and I do not know if I did what he said or if I only caused it to appear that way.

I jump when he barges into my room and it proves he's caught me about to do something I shouldn't be. I cower when he bellows and it proves he's caught me plotting my next escape. I can't hide anything from him, Dad says, so don't even try. He

can read my thoughts. He tells me what I'm thinking and then tests me to see if I'm telling the truth.
If I don't admit to what he knows already, I'm
lying. That's what hurts the most; when I lie to my
father.

My father *knows*. He *knows* things, he tells me. And
I have it written all over my face. He tells me I don't
have to hide because he already knows what I'm doing
and besides, he's my friend, he wants to help me. But
he can't help me if I keep lying to him. That's the one
thing I do that sends him into a blind rage and makes
him want to beat me to a bloody pulp: when I lie about
fucking around with men.

A country summer without leaving the hollow is
about the longest summer a sixteen-year-old girl can
get through. No phone calls, no visitors, no shopping
trips with Mom, no skating rink, no Jeff. My hair
stays long and dirty, I don't bother to wash it
anymore, let alone primp in the mirror with the curl-
ing iron. I dip in the pool, letting the chlorine strip it
of grease. On afternoons like this, when Mom and
Danny are in town and it's just Dad and me, the
country is deathly quiet. No music to punctuate the
air, no records for the turntable. I sneak down the hall
in my bathing suit, a towel wrapped around me, and
pad through the lush grass. I climb down the ladder

of the pool as quietly as possible and bob under the rim so my father won't know I'm out here. I don't want him to see me in a bathing suit. When I climb back up the ladder, I drape a towel down my front, chin to shin.

As the sun beats down on the roof of the metal trailer, I sit on my bed, sweltering and examine my fingernails. The tips used to peek out over my fingers as I rooted them to grow long like the other girls in school. But now they're peeled down to nubs, and I wait and watch, peeling them down the minute there's enough growth.

I spend the bulk of the day in silence, and monitor my father's face. If he looks a certain way, I may rush to confess what I'm thinking so he doesn't think I'm hiding from him.

But sometimes I can't catch my father's thoughts. And instead, they catch me.

With Dad tinkering in the garage, the farm dogs bark and barge to the edge of the yard, the hair on their backs razored up. I peek out the slats of my bedroom window and it seriously looks like there's a boy walking down the road. But no, it couldn't be. In all our years of living down here, I don't think anyone has ever walked down here by themselves. My thoughts race ahead. *Oh my God! I hope it isn't somebody to visit me. Dad'll kill me.*

I squint from my dark bedroom out the window into the bright summer sun.

Oh my God, it's that kid from art class who passed me a love letter on the bus.

I hurry to get dressed and try to stop him before my father does. I'm going to get it. I didn't even take that note seriously and besides the guy is a senior, he's way too old for me.

My father bellows, "Juulliiieee!"

I race down the hall and spring off the deck but it's too late. I round the corner of the trailer to the drive-way, my father steps out from the garage.

The kid stands in the drive, smiling hello.

Dad pulls out his gun and holds it drawn on the guy. "Who the fuck are you?"

The kid backs against the station wagon, parked in the drive, never taking his eyes off my father. "Uh, I know Julie from school, I used to ride the bus with her. I told her I might visit her over the summer."

No! Oh my God, that's the worst thing he could say. Dad's going to think I told him recently to come down. But I never invited him and, when he talked about visiting, it was back when we were still in school.

"Dad," I rush, "I swear, I didn't tell him to come down here. I haven't talked to him since art class."

"What's your name?"

"Mike. I ride the bus sometimes, I've been calling all summer but someone hangs up the phone."

"Mike, tell him. Tell him I told you not to come down here."

My father whips around, "Ah-ha, so you have been talking to this boy?"

"No!"

"Well, when did you talk to him? How would you know he was going to come down unless you picked up the phone in the house? Huh? See, I got you on that one, didn't I? How could you tell him not to come down if you're standing there claiming to not know that he was going to visit?"

I can feel my father's thoughts crest into a wave that looms over me. I am staring up into the foamy underside in those few hovering seconds before it crashes, drowning me.

"I'll tell you why. 'Cause your standing there lying to me, that's why." My father charges me with arms stretched out. He boxes my ears between his two massive palms, starting them ringing deep in my drums. They flash hot with pain and embarrassment.

I will never have the pearly pink fingernails of little girls.

I will never giggle in ditzy cluelessness.

I will never feel safe in my father's arms again.

* * *

149

I am made into the verbal punching bag and I soften to his blows, hoping if I am tender enough his hand will go straight through me. But he will punch no matter how hard or soft I become. He is so many different people inside. And I have to play name-that-tune with all of them, every moment a new record is placed under the needle of the jukebox.

As night falls, a bobwhite warbles in the distance and I whistle to him, long and slow. He sings back and I do it again, whipping him into a frenzy that makes me feel guilty when I'm called into the house. I can hear my mother's shrill voice pierce my love affair with the bird, tearing us apart. I climb the porch steps and his calls grow frantic, luring me back. I linger at the door and give him three final goodbyes. I'm pained to leave him. I am loved by this bird. Inside the trailer there are greasy dishes and my father's wet belch rising up from his chair.

I cannot remember what Jeff looks like. There is only the faint memory of the way he electrified my hair the night he touched it. I cannot remember what it's like to be a beautiful girl, a beautiful girl with all the world in her pocket. I stay in the trailer, under lock and key, under the watch of my father, day after day, crying out to bobwhite, my suitor in the trees. And the summer closes in around me down the long mile out.

Chapter Seven

The Indian summer breeze blowing down the dirt road brought with it hopes of fall. School would soon start and the end was near. The tawny leaves rustled in the wind's wake, marking the change of seasons. In a few short weeks the air would be laced with the chill of winter and the trees rooted upward in the hillside above would explode in crimson and gold, raining down leaves from higher ground onto the roof of the trailer, covering the fields in velvet patchwork.

I don't have to ride a roller coaster to feel my stomach drop. With the imminent fall comes the first day back to school, of walking the halls, clutching books to my chest, shifting my eyes from boys who stare and searching for any familiar face to latch onto. By the end of this first week, I'll know if the kid from art class squealed about Dad boxing my ears. I brace for kids to laugh or whisper as I walk past. But, more importantly, I'll know if Jeff has sent a message for me through one of the other kids who might have gone roller skating at the rink over the summer.

Homeroom is in Science this year. I head to the back of the class and grab a chair at the last lab table. I'm so lucky my only friend Carmen signed up for the same class first period. Three other girls sit at the second-to-last table and the five of us get grouped into lab partners. Whispering in the drone of the teacher, we swap stories of the summer. I tell the girls I mostly lounged by the pool and tried to grow my nails. Carmen leans over and wiggles her finger for us to come close.

"Is everyone here still a virgin?"

Everyone blushes, looking to one another.

"Thank God," Carmen sighs. "I thought I was the last one left."

The closest one girl got was putting her hand on *it*.

We're all virgins; scared of losing it, scared of dying this way.

And right there in science class, the V Club is formed. "V" for Virgin. Five girls sworn to secrecy, bound to tell one another in homeroom the day after it happens. A hand is slipped out into the middle of the lab table and, one by one, we all slide our own over the other, stacking them up. It is our bond as virgins. We don't know what it feels like on the other side, but we're all secretly hoping it's better than this. And with the pact made, an unspoken race is on between us. For as each of us agrees how special the first time should be, deep down none of us wants to be the last V standing.

The school year flies past, October, November, December, January and one by one the members of the V Club graduate by walking out of school on a Friday still a member and walking, transformed, into home-room on Monday. We can spot it from the door. We don't even have to say a word, we just thump a knee or tap a shoulder of the other girls so all of us look to the graduate and every time, she busts out laughing. We huddle over a dissection tray, the reek of formalde-hyde filling our noses as we listen intently to the details as they're shared. I watch their faces, so different to the girls in my father's magazines. I drink in the stories of their first time. One flips back a lock of hair to reveal a prune-coloured hickey sucked on her neck. Another tells us how big the boy was and how she didn't have any idea what she was going to do with it. The third girl says she didn't even know it was over until he started getting dressed – that's how lame it was.

There are only two members left: me and Carmen. Half the school year is over and the feeling is that school will let out for summer and we'll be left behind. Our prospects don't look good.

We joke about being last, about how we'll be spinsters in our seventies, living together, still virgins. We say; if it happens, it happens.

Before Carmen, I had another best friend; the new girl on the bus named Tammy, who sat next to me on her first day. Her family had moved down to the country from the big city of Columbus and by the end of seventh grade she was already wearing eyeshadow in rich shades of brown and cream just like the models in *Young Miss* magazine.

While Dad was in the hospital that summer, I begged Mom to let Tammy come down to swim in the pool. We dragged the plastic tube chaise longues into the yard and I brought out a can of lard from the kitchen, scooping it from the can to run down our delicate shins so they would tan darker. And I never before felt like such a teenage girl – a girl preening with my girlfriend, flipping through fashion magazines, talking about boys! We flicked our feet to the top countdown music station I'd tuned the radio to with the help of a coat-hanger wrapped around the antenna and stuck up in the sky.

I saw Mom before I heard her; her face appeared like a shroud through the crank-out window above the kitchen sink, she pressed her nose to the screen to see us better and that's when I saw her scowl. I sat straight up.

"Julie, get your ass in here!" she shouted, trying to get out of the house to reach me.

I jumped up and ran across the yard in my bathing suit but it was too late. Mom was struggling with the patio screen door that led out onto the deck; it had come off the track again. She had asked Dad a million times to fix it and now he wasn't here to yell at.

I ran faster, hoping I could counter her anger and get the door open; I would die if she screamed at me in front of Tammy. I made it to the bottom of the steps when she burst through the door, the cheap aluminium frame crumpled open by the knarled man's hands of my mother.

She flew down the steps and out into the yard, smacking her hands around my head and face. I flung my arms overhead and ducked as if swarmed by bees.

"What the fuck do you think you're doing?" she screamed. "There are fucking piles of dishes in the kitchen. You're out here with you little fucking friend, doing nothing?" She had hurt her hand hitting me, and that just made her madder. "You think you can lay around all day while I slave in that sweltering kitchen? Get in there and do those dishes."

Mom turns to my friend, sitting straight up and concerned. "Okay, missy, your time is up. You've caused enough trouble for one day. Get in there and call your mother to come get you."

The following Monday on the bus to school, Tammy sat next to me and we rode in silence.

"Don't worry about it," she said, my eyes stinging with tears. "You can come over next time. My mom's nice."

And it was Tammy, my once best friend, who passed me the folded note that said her older brother wanted to ask me to the Sweetheart Dance in February.

While I rode the bus to school, Brad was already driving to it. He wore Coke bottle glasses that hovered like magnifying lenses before his eyes, making them look separate, larger than the rest of his face, which was thick and pocked with the scars of acne. But he was a senior on the football team and wore a school jacket with leather sleeves of burgundy and white, Logan Elm's mascot colours. He hung out in the hallways leaning against the radiator with the bad boys of school, the country hicks who chewed tobacco and spat it into cups they carried around with him and the boys who picked fights in the hallways. But how bad could he really be in those glasses? I felt sorry for him. But even if he wasn't the best-looking guy, he was still the only person who might ever get me out of the house.

Dad says I can go to the dance but the boy has to come to the house and meet him first.

Brad offers to take me out on a few dates before the Sweetheart Dance so Dad can get to know him better. He pulls in the drive and walks up the gravel walkway, knocking gently on the pressboard door. He strides across the living room to shake Dad's hand.

"Nice to meet you, Sir."

"You're the neighbour boy, live down by Holiday Haven?"

"Yes, Sir."

"Well, you kids have a good time. Be back before curfew." My father looks over his glasses and shakes a finger. "You remember what happened last time."

"She thought she could fool her old man." He laughs out loud.

There's only one more week before the big dance. Brad comes down to get me for another date. With Brad so distorted behind his thick magnifying lens, we spend most of the time just driving with the radio on into small towns to cruise or hit McDonald's. I've never felt the electricity or love as I did with Jeff. I'm just getting out of the house with my old friend's brother. Brad offers Dad the exact location of the restaurant he's taking me to tonight. Dad motions from the chair that he's trying to listen to the TV and waves us out.

At the top of the road, Brad turns right, leading us away from the restaurant and deeper in the country. At first I think he got confused, or is so blind he doesn't know which way he's going.

"We were supposed to go the other way," I offer.

"I just have to stop off at my old house and pick something up for my mom."

He slows to pull in to the drive and cuts the engine when he stops at the deck. I wait in my seatbelt.

"Come on," he says getting out of the car, "this might take awhile." He smiles and his cheeks puff up over his eyes. I stand beside the car, not knowing what to do.

"Go on in, I'll be there in just a minute, the door should be open."

I walk up the steps of the deck and watch over the banister as Brad rummages through the truck of his car.

"Go in," he shouts from over the boot, "I'll be there in a minute."

Tammy's house has sat empty since her family moved. The "For Sale" sign has perched at the end of her driveway since before they were gone. The house is down a long driveway and can't be seen from the road. Not too many people want to live this far out and fewer still are willing to drive back here to look at the place.

The first room inside is the empty living room. The moon shines through the windows, giving it the illumination of a night light. My breath crystallizes, it's beyond freezing in here.

I look down the hall, towards Tammy's old bedroom. I visited her once in this house on a Saturday, after she saw Mom beat me in the yard. We lay on her bed, flipping through one of her mother's fashion magazines.

"Wait here," she said and leaped up.

I looked at the fashion models with make-up and beautiful hair, perfect white smiles and pretty pink nails. Some were girls the same age as me but we couldn't be farther apart. I wondered what it would be like to shop in a mall, to go to an afternoon matinée movie with my girlfriend or write a love letter to a boy. Aren't all girls supposed to do that when they're sixteen?

Tammy's hiss from the hallway called me and we snuck in the bathroom. She flicked on the light.

"Shhhhh," she said when I looked at her mother's expensive department store cosmetics splayed out like a make-up artist's.

She swept a fresh ivory eyeshadow applicator over a silken dial of shadow and I fluttered my eyelid shut. I could feel the coolness of the colour smooth over my eyelid and could not believe the way it shimmered in the mirror. She almost had a whole new face of make-up on me when footsteps led down the hall to the door.

"Tammy," her mother shouted. "You better not be doing what I think you're doing."

The doorknob jostled. "Why's the door locked? Open up right this minute."

Her mother twisted the doorknob and rushed in the bathroom. Her eyes flashed from her cosmetics to me. Her hand shot out and she smacked Tammy hard across the face. She hit her harder. My friend reeled back and almost fell in the tub. A red outline of her mother's fingers shone on her cheek but she did not cry, even in humiliation. Tammy's dad drove me home and the next day she got on the bus and sat in a different seat. It was too much, too close that her mother was just like mine. We held an unspoken pact never to reveal what happened, for what we might have said about one another was also our own truth.

"Hey," Brad startles me in the dark living room. "I'm here."

I turn around to see him just inside the front door, his back to me. He fishes something from his front pocket and I hear the deadbolt lock on the door click.

A dark lump is stuffed under the arm of his school jacket.

My heart races.

He turns around, the hulk of his shoulders silver lined by the moonlight.

Walking towards me, he parachutes the blanket under his arm by its edge and it falls crumpled like a disturbed picnic. "Lay down."

Brad's voice is hard in a way I've never heard it before. He's always talked sickly sweet and been so ass-kissing to my father that I didn't really take him serious.

"I said lay down on the blanket," he orders.

The floor is freezing, my teeth chatter. *Maybe we're going to make out, maybe the cold is just distorting his voice.*

Brad takes his glasses off. He leans on top of me and slobbers rather than kisses my mouth. He launches straight into it soap opera style so that I can't even kiss back. Squishing the back of my head against the floor with his face on mine, he slides his hand down my belly and fumbles with the snap of my jeans. Brad sits up with a start and before I can, he yanks off my jeans by the skinny ankles. Goosebumps race over my legs.

I can see his face in the faint light, his eyes nearly sealed, his swollen lids knitted like a mole. His skin is pocked like tough leather hide from chronic acne and I know he can't even see me.

I can't believe it. I wanted it to be different. But I guess he is taking me out to dinner. And besides, I say to quell my fear, I don't want to be the last V standing.

Brad spreads his arms like the wings of a hawk, me the prey beneath them. He perches on his palms, his thuggy arms locked at the elbows, flanking me on either side. His wide shoulders fill the window and block the thin shreds of moonlight that might shine upon me. I focus on the shadow cast by his body lifting in and out of my fixed gaze of vision.

I hold my eyes closed. I can't bring myself to look at his face. I do not want to see his tongue sticking out in concentration or his eyes rolling back in his head. He perches on spread fingertips, a bead of sweat drips somewhere from above.

When I open my eyes, I'm alone. The living room is dark, white noise fills my head.

"We better go." He appears above. "Get dressed."

I step outside and see him below, stuffing the blanket back into the trunk of his car.

He drives in silence and my brain floods, *think, think*. I don't know how to get a reading on him like I do with my father. I hope it isn't like this all the way to the restaurant.

As we crest the curve, he brakes at the last minute and turns into the dirt hollow that leads back home.

I stare out the window, wracking my brain with something funny or clever to say, anything to get him to talk to me.

But Brad stares out over the steering wheel and doesn't look over once.

He pulls into the drive and I linger at the open passenger door, feeling stupid.

"See you at school tomorrow?" I say.

"Yeah." He leans across the seat toward me. "And hey, babe, if you see me with the guys tomorrow, come up and say 'hi', let's talk about what we're wearing to the Sweetheart dance."

And everything's all right again. He bridged the gap. I was just thinking too much. Of course we're still going to the dance, that's why we went out tonight. He's shy, he just isn't much of a talker. But he still wants me. And that's all the matters.

"Hi, Sissy," Dad says from the cocoon of his chair. "I like that Brad, he seems like a nice boy."

My face sears with flush. But the living room is dark and my father, wrapped up in a sitcom, has not noticed that the half-hour show he is watching now is the same that was on when we left.

* * *

In the light of dawn, I wait for the bus and I'm no longer a virgin. As soon as I step onto the bus, I can feel it in everything. I see the kids who are already on and I know who is and who isn't. I watch new kids get onto the bus and I know who is and who isn't.

A throng of students pours in the front door of school and, even though I walk among them, I can tell who is and who isn't, just by a sixth sense.

I walk into homeroom. Carmen howls, reading the signs sparking off me. I laugh like the girls before me have and the only one left now is Carmen. I can read in her face that, although she's happy for me, she feels like any of us would, to be the last one.

Even though I couldn't look at my date, I'll tell the story as if I had. The girls lean in, eager for the details and I suddenly graduate, leaving my best friend behind.

When the bell rings and science class is over, I scurry through the halls to my next class. The senior boys sneer and I could swear there is a whisper they're hissing out to me. I haven't seen Brad today but can't wait to find him.

Brad lounges at the radiator with the same group of boys, he smiles at me and waves me over. The guys slap high fives and cheer.

He stretches his hand out and slips a finger through my belt loop, jerking me against his waist.

"Hey, Brad," a boy leaning against the radiator sneers. "You going to the Sweetheart dance?"

"To that stupid sissy hop? I wouldn't be caught dead at it," he says.

An alarm goes off in my head. "I thought we were going," I falter. "We're going to the Sweetheart dance together, right?"

Brad laughs and the gang of boys follows suit, slapping high fives.

"It all came down to the bet, sweetheart," Brad sneers. "Ha, get it? Sweetheart for the Sweetheart dance?"

I'm reeling.

"The bet was I could pop your cherry before the dance and I wouldn't have to go with you."

The guys erupt in hoots and hollers.

"Looks like I won the bet," he sniggers to the kid next to him and pushes his thick glasses up his greasy nose. I back away from the boys, my mouth open. I run toward the girls' locker room, the boys clap and cheer in my wake.

I curl myself in the enclave of the tile shower and slip down the wall, hugging my books. I wanted it to be so special. I thought he was my boyfriend. I thought he loved me. I felt sorry for him. He wasn't even good looking.

I wander like a zombie through the rest of my day. *Kids are cruel. Boys just want to stick their thing in your thing. There are guys out there that will slit your throat and leave you for dead. Trust me.*

And that's what makes me break down and sob. I don't want to know the men of my father's world and I made a pact with God that I wouldn't have to.

When the bell rings, I cling to the inside walls, letting the sea of students carry me to the next class. It's the last one of the day and two of the meanest guys in school are in the class with me. The same ones I swear I've heard hissing at me in the hallways.

"Zozips grego, nozips grego," one whispers from behind a cupped hand over his mouth. The other cracks up.

I watch the clock tick down until class is out and this horrible day will be done. I pivot in my seat, ready to dart out the door when the bell rings.

"The whole school knows, slut," Mean Boy One says from behind,

"'No Lips'. 'No Lips Gregory' that's your new nickname," the other laughs.

I don't know what they're talking about.

"Don't you get it? Brad says you ain't got any lips. He says you ain't got nothing between your legs like the girls in *Penthouse*."

I run crying, déjà vu in a recurring nightmare; boys are chasing me and I can't find the right bus to get on. The yellow buses pull away from the school and only the boy's car is left in the lot; feathered roach clips hanging from rear-view mirror of a white Trans-Am. I hang my head and whisper Tecumseh's prayer, *From where the sun now stands, I will fight no more forever.*

At the start of my last year of high school, I'm seventeen and Danny is only ten. Even though the gap between our ages seems greatest then, I still feel protective and close to my brother. I'm going to miss him like crazy when I leave home. And it's going to be so hard for him to not have me around. We cry together over what it's going to be like. How will he handle things by himself or break up the fights? I tell him I'll stay as long as I can but, as soon as I'm eighteen, I'm going to want to get out. He can call me anytime, day or night, I promise, and I'll come running.

It is during the fall, that Mom and Dad finally separate. Mom starts spending time with an older man who lives down the road on the way to town, a horseman with a cowboy's swagger and a fresh line of bullshit on just about anything. He asks her to help him with his pony rides at the seasonal fairs that happen in the fall, hitching the animals up to the walker and helping the kiddies on and off. Mom explains it'll be extra money coming in and Dad's just happy to see her gone for a few days.

It's only later when she's home that it dawns on Dad.

"Where'd you sleep?" he asks.

"In the camper, Dan." Mom sighs.

"Well, where'd he sleep?"

"Dan, you're just being crazy. He slept in the camper too, you idiot."

"This camper?" Dad says, looking in the door at the miniscule bunk.

Dad paces. Danny and I hear shouting from inside the house and rush out.

"For crying out loud, Dan." Mom slaps her leg. "He can't do anything." She stammers. "He, well, he you know, got kicked by a mule, it doesn't work."

Dad grabs Mom around the neck with his meaty hand and strings her off the ground.

"Heeeeelppppp," she hollers.

Danny dashes into the camper and jumps out of the door. He has a gun in his hand. He shoves into Dad and stands on his toes, leaning against him, then thrusts the gun into the base of Dad's skull, screaming at the top of his lungs. I stare at my little brother, stunned. He sprang to the task with the velocity of a man, with a strength I never knew existed in him. Like something inside was building up his whole life for this moment.

Danny holds in his boy's fist a clump of my father's hair. Dad screams for him to shoot him, to put him out of his misery. Mom screams at him to shoot Dad, to rid her of the asshole that ruined her life. Danny screams back, "Shut the fuck up, both of you. I'm not going to shoot Dad!" He looks to me, frozen in the yard and commands me to run down the road to the old neighbour's trailer at the bottom.

It is Danny who has taken control. I do as he tells me and sprint out of the yard, toward the neighbours. Out on the road, I turn back around one last time, to make sure Danny's okay. He still holds the gun to my father's head and the three of them stand by the camper. I feel like a girl for the first time in my life, a girl who has a man to protect her. No longer the one to save the family, I can now be the one who runs for help.

The time has come for me to leave. My beautiful brother is barely able to muster a smile, and veins along his temple pulse in and out, telling the true workings of what lies underneath. I feel so bad leaving him. He has to stay, while I am free.

"I wish I could take you with me, Danny."

"Me too, Sis," he cries. "Me too."

Chapter Eight

At 19, I live alone. I hitchhike to the big city of Columbus and land a job as a canvasser for an environmental group. I have no high school diploma, no money from Mommy and Daddy, just a driving will to escape.

At every turn, my girlish wiles are hidden behind a façade of male identity; I dress loosely in men's trousers, wearing threadbare old man's striped boxers beneath. My hair is long and sexy and my eyes stare straight ahead, but can flash a smouldering sexuality, depending who they fall upon. I wear cut-off jean shorts with a Swiss Army knife attached to my hip. My blonde hair is pulled up in a windswept bun, then anchored with long spikes of white animal bone that could double as weapons. For every soft hint of girl there is a razor-sharp edge I can pull like a switch-blade if cornered. I am neither feminine nor masculine but a melding of the two, pliable on the inside, metal shell on the outside, able to snap down and slice your finger off if you reach too fast for me.

All the world's a threat; men leer in doorways, men follow me with their eyes down the sidewalk, men stalk me in the grocery store. *Hey, baby, nice ass*, they whisper from behind as I squeeze for ripe oranges. They chase me on the highway, speeding to steady their car alongside mine, mouthing *pull over, pull over,* pointing to the shoulder. I have fine-honed their own male traits to repel them; I am an excellent spitter; if a man licks his lips when he sees me, I avert my eyes, then hawk out the window at his car. I can play pinball with the best of them, beating the machine with my fists, swearing like a sailor, bucking the levers with a thrusting hipbone. I can walk into the hardest junkyard in the worst part of town and talk shop with the men behind the counter and they will not treat me like prey. They wouldn't dare. I am roughhewn beauty, my face rote with the hard line of trouble. Every ounce of sensuality in me laced up with the leather strap of masculinity. I take pride in the fact that I don't date and everywhere I go I leave men hanging and hungry. My sense of control is a meagre badge hard won from a life stripped of being a girl; keeping my

172

beauty under glass, knitting a permanent crinkle in my brow to keep the wolves at bay. And deep down inside, all I want to do is walk in red high heels.

"Sis?" My brother's voice cracks eerie and hollow over a payphone line.

"Danny?" I groan from a deep sleep. "Are you okay? It's three o'clock in the morning."

My brother starts to cry.

"Danny? What's going on? Where are you?"

"I'm in Texas."

"Texas?" My brother is only thirteen and a half. "Is Dad with you?"

"Yes, and no."

"What happened?"

"Dad's in jail." My brother breaks down.

"Oh my God, do you have a place to sleep? Are you safe? Is anybody out there with you?"

"I'm sleeping in the truck. Dad pulled his fucking gun on this mechanic because they couldn't fix the air conditioner and the cops came and threw him in jail."

I calculate. Danny doesn't have a driver's licence. He's alone in Texas, sleeping in the cab of the truck he isn't even legally allowed to drive while our father is held on bail. Hitched to the back of the truck is a four-car trailer loaded with cars Dad has agreed to deliver and poor Danny, if he has to drive even between places

173

to park and sleep, will have to navigate the rig through city streets. Knowing Dad, there probably isn't a dime to their name until the cars get delivered. I want to reach through the phone and scoop up my little brother.

"Oh, Danny" I sigh. "I'm so sorry."

"I'm so fucking pissed, Sis." He buckles.

"I know, Danny, I know."

"What the fuck, why does he have to go and do this shit?" My brother cries bitter tears. His voice distorts from the way his mouth twists when he's angry, a trait he gets from our mother. He is so mad he could probably pummel Dad to a bloody pulp. But he won't. Neither of us ever will. We are both hardwired with a protective gene towards our father, for every intense negative emotion that arises, another equally intense one of sorrow or guilt cancels it out. And we cannot tell Mom. She will delight in threatening Dad to get full custody of Danny.

"You need money?"

"I don't have any to post Dad's bail."

"How much do you need?"

"I'm at a payphone, trying to find a lawyer in the yellow pages. I have to find out how much his bail is."

I sit in the dark and wait for my brother's call back. I can wire the money easy enough but I'd bus it all the way cross-country to give my little brother peace, to

wipe away his tears. The guilt is sinking me. I promised Danny I'd come running if ever he needed me.
I'm finally free. And it's my little brother who's now
his father's keeper.

That summer of being 21, my phone rings.

"Julie?" Mom rushes, "Thank God I caught you."

Mom is famous for this; calling in a panic with some
sort of drama she wants me to react to or rescue her
from.

"Now, Julie, listen to me." Mom licks her lips.
"This-is-ver-re-im-por-tant. I don't know if you're
going to believe this but." She pauses for dramatic
effect. "Your father is trying to kill me."

Sigh. According to my mother, someone is always
trying to kill her.

"Do you hear me?"

"Yeah, Mom," I sigh. "I heard you."

"I got something to send you. It is crucial, Julie,
crucial," she stresses, "that you do not open this envelope when you get it. Put it in a safe place. My God,
do not open it. If you opened it, it would be worthless."

Even with the receiver held away from my ear, I can
still hear her ramble on.

"I was out weeding the garden. Since your father
abandoned me, I have all this work to do around here
by myself."

I roll my eyes. She runs off with the neighbour man and kicks Dad out, and she says he abandoned her.

She continues. "And a car came down the road real slow. It stopped across from the manger and the window rolled down, you know they had one of those automatic windows that lowers with the button," she says, "and I swear there was the barrel of a sawed-off shotgun aimed right at me. I screamed and ran into the horse shed. Thank God they drove off. Now listen to me. Listen. To. Me. If anything, *anything* happens to me your father's probably the one who did it. I want you to go straight to the police with that envelope I'm sending you. Okay? This is very important. Do you understand?"

"Yeah, Mom, I got it."

"Promise me, Julie, promise me you'll keep it from your father."

"Sure, Mom, whatever you want, I'll do it."

And so a large manila envelope arrived in my mailbox, scrawled with my mother's chicken-scratch cursive, *DO NOT OPEN!* Mom had double-scotch-taped it closed for added security.

I threw it under the kitchen cabinet where I kept the mismatched Tupperware containers she handed down to me and all the other junk in my kitchen. And there it sat for seven years.

* * *

Even though Mom is married to the horseman now, she still stalks my father. She drives past where he stays to see if he's home and bangs on the door if other cars are parked outside.

"Dan, open the door right now!" Mom screams.

"Go away," my father says from the inside.

"Adulterer! Adulterer!" she shouts outside to whoever might be on the sidewalk.

It's testament to Mom's sense of entitlement that she sees Dad as owing her for walking out. Mom moved her horseman into the home Dad spent his life working to pay for and he slinked away crying. He gave her everything; the land and the trailer, the camper and the truck, the Batmobile boat and of course, his garage. All bought with his paycheques while taking almost nothing for himself. And the few things he did love, he lost those too. When he walked away, it was with the clothes on his back. In the seventeen years they were married, that's all Dad managed to accumulate. My father moved into a rundown garage on the main drag of a nearby small town and tried to begin a life. He went into the army at only seventeen and met Mom when he was nineteen. My father had never really lived on his own before.

Since then, a steady stream of low-brow girlfriends had graced the La-Z-Boy in my father's apartment. The latest is missing her two front teeth and my father jokes in front of her about the benefit of having a toothless lover. She laughs.

Mom sits in her truck outside Dad's garage apartment, engaging in a useless display of emotion. Danny calls to say she's locked herself in the cab with a bottle of pills and is threatening to commit suicide if Dad doesn't talk to her. To this my father barked from his chair, "Let her."

"Sis," Danny begs, "Can you please come help me with this?"

True to my word, I get in the car and drive down there.

Armed with a magazine I waggle on the other side of the window, I lure Mom into unlocking the door. I can't understand how after all those years of fighting and violence and misery and her being married to a new man, she is now suicidal because Dad will not take her back.

I remind her of all the hard times that went down on Burns Road and ask her why she wants him to want her.

"Because," Mom wails, "if that no-good, faggot-assed, wife-beating, paranoid-crazy, cocksucking son of a bitch don't want me, who will?"

* * *

My mother is moving to Montana. She has given up her horseman husband and is going to shack up with an Indian named Hue in his trailer on the reservation.

Dad agrees to move her cross-country, loading up all her furniture and pets to drive her four states from Ohio. Anything is worth it, he reasons, to get her out of his hair.

With our mother finally gone, my father turns destitute. He sits in his chair and, in addition to the eighteen hours of daily television, he calls me on the phone and sighs, heavy and deep, into the receiver.

At 22, I have a better paying job and work for myself. I have Dad drive to Columbus to meet me. He can come along on the sales calls I'm making today for my job. He arrives at my door in a raunchy T-shirt with a monster truck on the front that says, *Injection is nice but I'd rather be blown.*

"Dad," I groan. "Why do you have to be so gross?"

"What? You don't like my T-shirt, Sissy? I think it's funny."

In the store, I say hello to Yvette, the owner, who has a hippy shop that sells feminist books, incense and leather-bound journals stamped with fairies and Celtic symbols. My father inspects a shelf of T-shirts, slicing them one by one around the curve of the bar, reading the slogans that splash across the chest.

He pulls one out with the image of a car garage on the front and reads aloud, "*Lube shop, free hand job while you wait.*" My father howls with laughter.

Yvette walks from behind the counter to find one she wants to show him. "Check out this one for *Greasy Dick's Repair Shop.*" And my father cackles till he cries.

Yvette gives me her jewellery order from behind the counter and stands at the register with her long grey hair hanging to her waist, both delighted that my father has this ill sense of humour about him and surprised that I am this man's offspring. They are both pear-shaped and boisterous cacklers. And I hate to say it but love is in the air.

On the way out, my father sheepishly approaches Yvette behind the counter, checking out a girl buying a Mother Earth necklace. "Yvette, um, would you like to go to dinner with me tonight?"

Without a beat, Yvette blares to a store full of customers, "I have a Cocaine Anonymous meeting at seven but you can pick me up after that."

They both hoot with laughter.

My father calls me days later, floating on cloud nine. Life has turned into something he never knew possible. He shares secret rendezvous dates in the parking lots of Bob Evans with his new girlfriend, my client. My father drives his ridiculous chopped-up van with the fold out bed in the back and they spend the evening making out and watching TV powered by a generator that runs off the diesel engine. Dad sticks a sign in the window: *If this van's a-rocking, don't come a-knocking*.

For the first time in my life, I witness my father in the delicate stages of love. He shows a childlike vulnerability and kindness, a soft spot I have never seen in him before. It makes me wonder if there was ever any love at all in the life he had with Mom. He showers to see his girlfriend, wears a splash of good cologne. He combs his hair, brushes his teeth and trims his wildman beard. He opens doors for her, pays for their dinners together and sends her a dozen roses just because. He walks dreamy through stores, picking out trinkets and fuzzy white stuffed puppy dogs. For the first time in his life, I think my father is in love.

But within a few months, things are crashing. Dad brings his loaded gun to Yvette's house. He takes it out of his pocket and lays it on the nightstand. She tells him not to bring it again, she has children and grandchildren and they are in and out of the house, she doesn't want a loaded gun lying around. They argue. He refuses to come without it. She refuses to let him stay. And one day, just like that, she stops taking his calls. My father calls her from his phone, my phone, a payphone, trying to win her back. I call her on his behalf but she tells me he isn't going to change. He calls me right away to ask what she said. I tell him that she said she loves him but can't accept his need to carry a loaded weapon. My father is heartbroken, but the lie I sandwich with the truth leaves a streak of hope in his heart. And with hope, he breaks down on the phone in my ear. My heart aches for him. I wish I could win her back for him. She changed his life, she made him happy. But my father cannot understand. And I cannot explain it to him. I was raised inside his paranoia but people on the outside word weren't. Where I walk a tightrope between the two worlds, my father lives in just one.

I can't remember fighting with my brother in the backseat as a kid or any other normal childhood banter. The days of our childhood were spent on pins and needles skating around our parents; each of us living as different lives as possible from one another. Where I had things light, my brother had them worse. Where things were hell for me, he wasn't even aware there was anything wrong.

Our bond is strongest now, with me age twenty-four and him just seventeen. My job taking orders for a jewellery company sees me making enough to slip my family the extra. I take him shopping for cool jeans and help him clean the windowless room in the back of the garage where he sleeps on a mound of clothes on the floor. I will sacrifice my rent to provide for my brother. I buy him a bed and towels. I want him to have the best clothes and the special knick-knacks a teenage boy might want in his life: a wall hanging of his favourite band, an electric blue lava lamp, a package of six pairs of new socks, everyday stuff my father doesn't think to provide for him.

And on Christmases I feel even more responsibility to give, not just to my brother but to my Dad as well. There is deep compassion wired into me for my father; I feel sorry for him and laugh at his corny jokes so he isn't as aware of his loneliness. I reflect back to him that he is perfectly normal and shovel load after load of light into his bottomless pit. I take any kernel of kindness he shows and magnify it to the ninth degree.

It's the first Christmas after Mom has moved. The weight of not having to tend to her over the holiday has relieved the usual dread of getting together with everyone. The joy in both my father and brother for the same reason is undeniable. It's the first year Dad has an official girlfriend who has stood the gun test. It's the first year Danny will not have to placate our mother and the first year I won't have to babysit her.

My car isn't running but still I have bought all the Christmas presents for Danny and Dad; excited to play Santa Claus.

Dad is coming to Columbus with my little brother to collect me Christmas morning, then we'll head back down to the garage where they live to open presents. I sit on the couch and wait, clipping pictures of flowers grown from bulbs in a plant catalogue. I dream of planting bulbs in the spring and watching flowers come up, multiplying each year, roots fingering down into the ground. A horn sounds outside.

The car is from a fleet my father got at an auction and is without a back seat. I sit on my brother's lap, my back curved into the windshield, my butt shoved up against the glove box. Danny and I are close. And he's still my little brother; I can tickle him so forcefully he wets his pants. He is just a dork at the age of seventeen, with his porky jawline and post-adolescent acne. On impulse, I reach out and run a finger over one of his blemishes, a giant blackhead that begs for freedom. I remember my mother and shiver, the way she towered over me in the bathroom, picking my face.

Dad says his new girlfriend will be spending the day with us.

"What's her name, Dad?"

"Oh, don't ask," Danny quips.

"Biggerin." Dad laughs, "I call her Biggerin."

"I don't get it."

"Well, she's big. Bigger than a house."

"Get it?" Dad prompts, "Biggerin a house." And does his trademark howl.

Her real name is Carol and she sits in her very own La-Z-Boy chair back at the garage apartment. There is a small stack of presents under an artificial tree that looks like it's been pulled out from under the muffler of the car that ran over it. Silver tinsel drapes in clumps off its spindly branches. Danny and I haul in the stash of presents I brought.

Danny has the most, between me buying for him and Dad's new girlfriend, then Dad comes in a close second. I sit and pass out presents from a big pile while a few make their way to me. Danny oooh's and ahhh's at the onslaught of gifts, Carol loves the things Danny and I got for her. I unwrap a few non-specific gifts from Carol as she doesn't really know me. My father hands me a small one, loosely wrapped. "Here Sissy, this is what I got you."

I savour the unwrapping. It's a G.I. Joe children's toothbrush. The price is still on the handle in the orange sticker: 99 cents.

"Heeyyy, thanks, Dad. You trying to tell me some-thing?" I joke. But I'm propping myself up inside. *Why do I ever think it's going to be different? When will I ever learn this is all I'm ever going to get?* That

Christmas was the first time it dawned on me how I toil to buy presents when I don't even have a car to drive.

My father opens a gift from his girlfriend, a board game called *Taboo*.

"This is my gift to all of you, to our family," Carole says.

"Have any of you ever played?" she wants to know.

Danny and I shake our heads "no".

"Ooooo, it's so much fun," she squeals, "Let's play right now. It's got all these raunchy questions. Your dad's going to love it."

My father pants like a puppy, hangs his tongue out.

Danny and I look at each other.

Carol sets the game up on the card table that doubles as the one they use to dine on in the kitchen and we fan around the board to play. My brother and I are one team and Dad and Carol are the other. Each person has to draw a card from the deck and ask the question on the card to the other team member of the opposite sex. If they answer, that team moves up the board, if the question is too "Taboo" and they don't want to answer, the other team moves up.

Carol goes first. "Okay, Danny, here's a good one. What is an erogenous zone?"

"I have no idea," my brother answers.

186

"Good, we get to move. Dan, your turn."

My father draws a card, reads it silently. Then howls.

"Sissy, how many times in a night," Dad looks at us over the card, "have you performed fellatio?"

My brother and I are horrified. I don't know what the word means and I don't think Danny does either, but we both know it's something a dad isn't supposed to ask his kids.

"Dad, I don't think we should play."

"It's only a game," Carol protests.

"It's not for families to play." I groan. "I mean, c'mon."

"Who plays this kind of game with their kids?" Danny snaps.

"You're no fun, Goober," my father says. "You're being like your mother; a stick in the mud."

When it's time to drive me home that night, we all load into another car from the fleet, one with a back seat and head up to Columbus, about an hour away. On the highway outer belt, the engine sputters as the car runs out of gas. We coast onto the shoulder and roll to a stop. The temperature instantly drops in the car and we sit in the dark as semi trucks barrel past, rattling the windows. Carol and Dad bicker in the front seat about who was supposed to fill up the gas tank. I watch my breath crystallize in the distant glow of a highway light and remember the countless times as a kid when an automobile Dad had hodgepodged together would break down. We might be stuck for hours until we could get on the road again. I wonder what Dad is going to do to get us heat and get me home.

"Hey, Sis?" Dad says to me in the rear-view mirror, "Would you want to take the gas can and go get us some gas?"

"Uh." I look out at the dark highway, cars and trucks zooming past feet from my door. "Okay."

"I think there's a flashlight in the trunk. Goober, get out and get her the flashlight. I'd do it but I think I might be coming down with a cold."

My father says to anyone in the car, "I think if you run across the highway to the other side, there's a gas station a couple miles back."

Danny and I stand on the other side of the highway in the dark with our thumbs out. I'm in the front, closest to the highway, he lags at the shoulder. As the girl, it'll be easier for me to snag a ride. A pickup truck flies past and, seeing me, taps on the brakes and pulls up ahead. We run toward the tail lights with the gas can and hop in the bench seat of the truck.

The driver looks over and sees a guy with me; a slight disappointment clouds his face. By the time he drops us off at the station a few miles up, he scratches his head confused. "And your dad is back in the car?" he asks.

"Yeah, he's got a cold."

The driver offers to wait while we fill up the gas can and take us back down the road, but we don't want to inconvenience him.

"I insist," the stranger says. "There's no way I'm letting a couple of kids go out on the edge of a highway on Christmas and hitch in the dark. I couldn't live with myself if anything happened to you two."

A half hour later, my father slows in front of my place and I climb out of the back seat of the car into the road. I watch them drive away, the belch of exhaust from the tailpipe spewing diesel dust, the muffler tied up with a coat-hanger, the gas can in the trunk. My father: the car mechanic, the fix-it-all guy, the provider.

In the span of six hours, I was given a child-sized toothbrush, accosted in a board game about sex and stuck out on the side of a highway to hustle gas for the family car. In the hours leading to midnight that Christmas, something shifted. Collected as a naïve girl, I was dropped back off a jaded young woman.

In the first grey months of the New Year, the shift over Christmas unearths dreams from the bottom of a well; dreams of my father chasing me, his rage unstoppable, fists in the air, gaining on me, my long high-water legs no match for his rhino speed. He is beating down my door, demanding I climb into the marital bed. *No!* I scream and try to squeeze through a tiny sliver of window. He is after me in a car, chasing me down the road while I drive like mad, pictures of flower bulbs I've cut from a mail order catalogue fluttering off the dash toward the open window as I clutch for them in the air.

I wake in bed, burning with anger.

I slip into a seasonless mentality, lying on my back watching shadows move across the ceiling, day to night, until I am dreaming awake and sleeptalking. I can take anything good in my mind and flip it. I can swing wildly out from centre, trying to capture the loose ends of my thoughts as they unravel; it can take me forever to get back to the middle. But I do not trace it back to my father. I need him to need me. I need to try to please him, make him happy, earn just a crumb of praise and notice. And even if something significant shifted in me at Christmas, the space between then and now has disappeared.

There are so many ways I'm like my father. A book falls in my apartment and I jump, easily spooked. I can't find the hairdryer. I look for signs of entry; a broken window, a door left ajar, how did they do it? I know I left it in the bathroom. I obsess as I walk down the sidewalk to the main street. *Who could have done it? Was it my neighbour? An old boyfriend who still has a key? The kid across the street?* My brain churns into knots over the missing hairdryer. A boy passes me on the sidewalk and steps to the side but doesn't look at me. *Do I look that bad? Why won't he look at me?* I turn around to stare, thinking I'll catch him looking back, but he's walked on.

My thoughts knit a deep furrow as my legs carry me out to the main drag. There are people, lights, a million different signs to interpret. I wait at the cross walk, watching cars roll by. I can hear laughter in one. It's a car full of students, driving by so fast I can barely see them. I look at my shoes. It's my shoes; they're laughing at my shoes. I put them on in a rush; they're the wrong ones for this outfit. I smooth down my clothes, synapses firing in my head. My hand flies up to my face, to shield me from the people around me, people I know are staring at me, laughing. I turn my back to the street and run home, leaning against the door once inside.

I yank the living room curtains closed. The cord to the hairdryer pokes out from under the couch.

How did they sneak it back in?

I stand in the middle of the dark room.

Didn't I lock the door when I left?

One shoe on, one shoe off.

Is someone watching me when I leave?

Hairdryer in hand.
Were they here while I was gone?
Smoke whisping from my ears.

In a corner of my mind is the small echo of how I used to be, a voice of reasoning not heard since I was fifteen and my father stole my *Leave it to Beaver* T-shirt. I secretly mocked him in my mind, gaining courage for the first time to question his perception, but I also wondered if people did think I was prostituting myself. It was enough doubt to blow a hole in my own reasoning, a hole I climbed through until I stood in Dad's world and saw myself through his eyes, through his mind. I stretched my own sanity out so thin it met his. Like millions of plankton floating towards me through the water, I could not tell my own thoughts from his suspicious ones. Left to twist my own threads, my father's paranoia became my own.

When a stranger laughs, I know they're making fun of me. I don't hear voices in my head, I hear real people, saying real things that I interpret as messages to decode. If I overhear two people in a store say, "I know, it's just disgusting," I'm sure they're talking about me and speaking loud enough to let me know. Now I have to figure out what's disgusting about me so I know what they're referring to. If a store clerk wants to see my ID when I'm checking out, I know it's because they don't believe I am who I say I am; they're calling me a liar.

And I react; throwing my weight around like full wet sandbags, socking people on the kneecaps. Like my father, I give the store clerk a hard time because I can. It's a bully instinct, fine-honed to second nature. In the back of my mind, I catch myself. I feel bad for snapping at people. I know at some point I will have to whittle away this instinct and pop the belligerent bubble that protects me.

Out on the street, I stop to fish gum from the bottom of my bag and catch my reflection in the glass. Despite how ugly I feel inside, my face holds an innocence caught off guard; a startling beauty that astounds me. I want to move with eloquence and grace through this life, as if on an escalator of ghosts. I want to shake from my being every way I learned to be like my father and pare myself down to the core, back to when I was just a girl, born on the day of Liberace, with hopes and dreams as pearly as pink nail polish.

I must loosen the holds of my own brand of crazy. My father's suspicious thoughts overlay my own, like a sheet of plastic melted to my skin. I'm wired like him; a stupid ballsy-ness, wrapped in dynamite. The barbs of my personality puncturing everything I touch. But I'm not him. I can hear my mother's lunatic ramblings

in my own run-on sentences. I see it in my face; pocked
with the half-moon thumbnails of my mother. How I
sink my teeth into a banana is exactly like her. But I'm
not her. I wish I could divorce myself. Instead of
getting the best of me, I got the worst of them both.

The panic I feel is the fear of my father, never exca-
vated, returning to me in my dreams. It is the fear that
if I ever truly needed him, he would crumble like a
sandcastle, something that looked so real but which I
could put my hand straight through. I rush to give so
there is never empty space between us. Because if he
never stepped in to fill it, my dread would be realized:
I never meant much in the first place. The ache in my
heart is for my father; it is me, driving like a banshee
after any old geezer in a classic car, chasing down his
ghost. Is it worse to have loved and lost a beloved
father or never to have had one at all?

In my family a good memory might be eating ham
salad sandwiches in a parking lot before we took our
ancient old boat that looked like the Batmobile out on
the lake.

I would cut out the part a half hour later where
Mom was screaming at the top of her lungs, her shrill
voice carrying over the water to other boaters and Dad
would be screaming back that if she didn't shut up, he
was going to hurl her off the boat in the deep end of

the water. I would selectively pass over this part of the memory and the heavy mood that hung like a thundercloud trailing overhead. In order to come away with the good memory of eating ham salad sandwiches in a park for ten minutes. I would have to cut and paste accordingly, with most of the day lying in cuts on the editing room floor. There was no one time in our family that I could not connect the dots from a good time to a knock-down drag-out fight. Nothing was free from the undercurrent of violence that ran through every moment of our lives.

The family I know uses my social security number to get credit cards, they forge my name on important documents, they take me out for my 25th birthday and forget to bring any money, then fight at the table over who should pay.

My father slams his fist down on paper placemats; guests around us halt their chewing. He looks ridiculous in his plastic Red Lobster bib, trying to retain order in the court, a hunk of chowder dangling in his beard like a rock climber. Mom, visiting from Montana, erupts in a string of obscenities, pushes back from the table so hard her chair topples over. It lays there on the floor like a tipped quadriplegic. She storms off to the ladies room to corner a new victim and garner sympathy, successfully ducking out of the bill while appearing to be justified. I pay for another bad seafood dinner with the family and smooth the seams. On the way out the door, my father asks the friend I brought with me for her phone number.

"What?" He balks at me, "She's free, white and 21."

They have given me their Christmas lists like I was Santa since I was a girl. They have hit me with their fists, kicked me in the gut, given me sneering titles so humiliating I have felt pierced with a knife.

On the way out of the restaurant, my parents say separately, "Happy birthday, Sis. I love you."

But I think I'm starting to get it. No one who loves me would treat me that way.

Chapter Nine

I do not need a roller coaster to feel my stomach drop. Alone on the side of a wet highway, I stand at the berm, getting sprayed by sludge. At 26, my car is one of the many I will own in my twenties, all of them death traps; gas gauges that spike to full when empty, heaters that blow out cold dust, voltage regulators that drain the battery, engines given to spontaneous sparks. On this particular day, my old car's gas gauge shows full and I've just run out.

A man pulls up slow behind the crippled car. He knows I'm out of gas; he's got some right here in the trunk. I hold down the hinged bottom of the licence plate above the bumper and he guides the long-ridged nozzle from the can into the hole. We are two sets of hands, our bent-over bodies working in a tight space. As he slides in the nozzle, he locks on my eyes, his thin lizard lips curl in the faintest of smiles. His breath is rancid with meat between molars and I am studied concentration, eyes glued to the task at hand. Time drags, there along the highway, and I arc the gas can to glug into my tank all the faster. The soft rain isolates us from the line of cars whizzing by. Even though there are people less than ten feet away, I am alone and he knows it. The rawness of my exposure, there for the taking, drops me. It is sealed in one singular moment, his eyes boring into mine as he slides the nozzle out and shakes off dribbles of gas. My boneless fingers slide from the plate; it snaps shut. I break from his hold and run to the driver's seat. *Please God, let this car start, please God.* He's at the driver's window, frozen open until I get the car started. Lunch? Just up at the diner at the gas station? Only take a little bit? I dart my eyes for exit ramps, there is only the car and the ditch, and after that a field that leads to nothing good. If I say no, he could make a grab for me. If I feign interest, I can make a getaway.

I say through the open window, "Follow me to the gas station. Let's make sure I have enough to get there."

My voice holds the hope he is looking for, the hope that calms him so he isn't temped to make a grab for me, the one that almost got away. I am willing him my time and that is enough for now.

The car sputters, coughs, but finally starts. I slam the lever down to get the window up and he presses in, frantic for me to roll it down again. I accelerate into the slow lane. The mile to the station is endless. Please God, don't let me run out of gas again, and he tails me the whole way. If I can just make it, I'll be around people, people I can run up and grab the arm of. I put three dollars in change in my gas tank and the man waits for me, parked at the mouth of the entrance, between my car and the road. I will walk calmly to his window and tell him I have to call my dad to let him know I'm okay. I will walk across the dirt lot to the payphone and slide the door closed behind me. I will pick up the receiver and pretend my ATM card is a calling card. I will talk into the dial tone of the receiver and animate my hands. I will stay in the phone booth and make facial expressions of conversation until he gives up and leaves. It will be our little secret. We both know I have no one to call.

The only thing that will make me safe: walls around me, exit ramps lined along my path, escape hatches, well-lit hallways, floodlights in the basement. I leave the lights on all the time to illuminate the dark world I know, lying wait right outside my circle of light. The dark world of men and danger, the narrow escape, the consider-myself-lucky times, the look on his face, the glint like a switchblade tip held to my jawline, the spark of violence that twinkles in his eyes, dancing them alive in fiery pupils. I know this world too well. Now, at 28, I keep all the lights on. Every single one.

On Father's Day, I sit in the basement of the old farmhouse I've rented on the edge of a ravine, sifting through the final bags of junk from my last move. My hand reaches into the bottom of the trash bag and I pull out the manila envelope Mom sent so long ago when I was only 21.

The envelope, stuffed under a kitchen cabinet in my old apartment for seven years, is bare at the edges and nibbled away on the flap by the mice from my old place. Splotches of urine watermark the envelope giving it the hue of piss yellow tie dye. I pick it up by the corner and begin to toss it in the trash can when I catch the faded scrawl of my mother's cursive hand: DO NOT OPEN.

Mom moved out of state years ago. She sent me this packet before she left, prompted by the idea that Dad had hired a hit man to kill her. She corralled him into moving her cross-country, then threatened to take away his disability if he didn't give her a portion of it every month. And throughout her life in Montana, she has continued to pose as his wife to claim the benefits of his excellent medical insurance. Needless to say, it seems Dad needs protecting from her. Gone five years, and she still tries to run this family from behind a curtain. Dad isn't going anywhere near Mom – let alone making plans to kill her.

I stare at the envelope as memories flood me. How mad it was back then, to take my mother's phone calls and listen to her crazy stories. To hang out at my father's garage while his junkyard buddies gawked at me in cut-off jean shorts, no wiser to the way I looked than a ten-year-old would be. I was just a scared girl back then, with no idea how to find my way or make my thoughts separate from my parents.

I'm curious what kind of circus drama exists inside this envelope, sent so long ago, with the promise it would answer all kinds of questions about Dad.

I peel away the yellow Cellophane tape Mom criss-crossed, overlapped and double sealed the envelope with. It seems so melodramatic. I open the top, sure I'm going to get a laugh out of some deranged letter Mom wrote, showing the state of her mindset.

There is a copy of her life insurance policy and a will she pecked out on a typewriter.

The first line reads:

I, Sandy Sue Duane, of sound mind and body.
Underneath, Mom has added an additional line: *I, Sandra Rainer, of sound mind and body*. Rainer was the horseman's last name. And yet a third line exists beneath the two. *I Sandy Gregory, of sound mind and body*. Her will instructs all the animals she has as pets to be put to sleep and for herself she requests a closed casket, and actually types: *So that people won't be standing around talking about how crazy I was.*

I shake my head. *My mother*. Remaining are five type-written pages, with Veteran's Hospital letterhead. They are pages dated from the time Dad was in the hospital. I sit on a plastic milk crate under the single bulb of the basement light and read the lines.

Page One:
This 36-year-old, white, married male is seen at the request of Dr L for diagnostic evaluation and evaluation of dangerousness. Examination reveals a large, boyish-looking man who is little more than moderately obese. His hair is short but unkempt and he has a beard, trimmed and flecked with gray. He is wearing a T-shirt, jeans and jogging shoes. Despite being put upon and negativistic, there is a boyish sort of dependency

about him that leads him to reach out to the examiner with some conciliatory humour and bid for sympathy in kind of a "What can you do in a situation like this?"

The patient ruminates a great deal before dropping off to sleep at night, sleeps 4 hours, then gets up. He has remarkable emotional liability and is occasionally close to tears, especially when talking about his family. He also presents a feeling of some concern, perhaps even some guilt, when he talks about having 22 jobs in the last seven years. He is in the hospital for a job-related hassle. There is a family history of alcoholism; "I am the son of a war bum." The patient was referred here after a hassle with his foreman in which the patient stormed out of the foreman's office and went up on top of the building to jump off. It turns out that the only way to the roof was through a co-worker's office and he talked him out of jumping. Beyond that the patient has been labelled by co-workers as "Just like that guy who killed all those people in McDonald's." It also turns out that he has physically abused his wife, gotten in numerous fist fights going to flea markets with friends of his, carries a .25 pistol and last pulled this weapon on "one of those things dressed in the mini-skirt … pretending it was a girl but it was a man."

Yeah, that's my dad. As an afterthought, I think about the description his co-workers gave, "Just like that guy who went into McDonald's and blew everybody away." I remember that guy from the news as a kid. He was scary. Was my dad scary like that to others? Did people see him as the same brand of crazy? Did they ever wonder if he had kids?

PAGE TWO:
Mr Gregory states that he was first hospitalized psychiatrically in 1966 for months. He reports that he was initially hospitalized because of problems with his middle ear but after there were negative findings in this regard he was placed on a locked psychiatric ward. He was again hospitalized in 1972 for a week after "I tried to kill myself."

This would have been when he stuck his head under the jack in the driveway. I was three then. Dad was depressed and suicidal and Mom made fun of him.

From July to October of this year he was hospitalized at a Chillicothe ward because "they think since I carry a gun all the time I'm homicidal." He reported that he did not bring his gun to my office because his wife would not allow him to do so. He says that he carries his gun so he "Won't get picked on." And continues "They ain't going to get me in a bank or a McDonald's and kill me." In mentioning this he is making one of his many references to the multiple murders in the McDonald's restaurants in California. His view of his mental health is "I don't think I have a problem but everyone else does. There are two sets of rules; one for everybody and one for me to help the niggers."

Page Three:
Mr Gregory says that he has noticeable mood swings. He said he was not depressed during our visit, but rather frightened. Having stated so, he cried. He says he cries frequently and that he first experienced auditory hallucinations in 1967 and that he has both visual and auditory hallucinations. About a week or two ago, there was "a little man on my shoulder saying the whole world's fucking with you." Typically his auditory hallucinations involve two men, "One says nice things, the other says bad things." When asked about suicidal ideation, he cried. He says he has made about 10 suicidal efforts. In 1972 he attempted suicide by hanging himself with a rope. He says in that same year he attempted to have his car roll over him,

but the car did not move. He says that he also went to a roof to jump when he was upset about work, but that a friend at the company talked him out of his intention to jump.

The patient lives out in the country to protect his children ages 15 and 7 from the corruption of the world. He cries when talking about his 15-year-old daughter and the possibility of incestuous relationship or incestuous fantasy needs to be explored. The patient has gone from one church to another because "When you go to church on Sunday, you have to go 4 times the next week and 10 times the next week … they never let you alone." Almost as an afterthought the patient wants to deal with "What are we gonna do about the voices?" He describes voices that have a histroid quality, men's and women's voices, telling him what he should do. They have never told him to harm anyone but have told him to kill himself. It appears that he has the wherewithall to commit murder and suicide with a Raven in his pocket.

I sit stunned. All that time I was scared of my dad in this way; to be in a bathing suit around him, to hide the natural parts of being a girl, of not wanting to be in close quarters with him and feeling guilty like it meant I didn't love him. But somebody else saw, saw what was happening. It's the first time I have seen any sign that it wasn't right for me to feel that way around Dad. It's the first time it dawns on me that it wasn't my fault.

THE NOTES CONTINUED:
There needs to be approached about possible incestuous relationship with the daughter and whether or not she is being kept as a "hostage" out on the farm.

Impression: Schizophrenic disorder, paranoid type, with major affective features.

"Hostage". The word burned into me. Someone who never met me suspected that Dad was holding me as a hostage down at the trailer. Just by interviewing him. They believed it enough to write it but they didn't do anything to help me.

All this time, I was alone in that reality. I tried to make it up to Dad, for betraying him. I took the punishment and gently unbraided his twisted thoughts if only to try to keep him from attacking me. I made sense of the paranoia and adjusted myself and the way I saw things in order to fill the gaps of insanity.

There on Father's Day, in a mice-encrusted manila envelope, were the five pages of truth that made everything make sense. All this time I had righted things in my head that kept tipping over. I believed Dad was fine, that the hospital stint was a ploy for money that fitted with Mom's big plans. I believed that if I could just have explained more quickly or been convincing enough that maybe I could have gotten Dad to understand I wasn't sneaking out the trailer windows, that I was scared of men and that I only wanted a nice boy who would hold my hand and make me feel safe. I believed that when he didn't understand it was my own fault. Because the faster I tried to explain, the more he thought I was lying, until I didn't know what the truth was anymore. I tried to be so convincing with the truth that it felt like I was lying, making up an elaborate story. That's how Dad saw it and I began to feel the same way about myself.

I was just a kid. A kid those same doctors, after writing those pages on my father, put on the stand at his hearing and asked loaded questions. They'd asked me those things in front of a man they thought was schizophrenic – then sent him home to me. No one followed up. They just turned him loose.

I sat bawling in the basement, holding the papers, lost in time. I cried for myself, for everything I went through that was part of loving my father, and for trusting him that there was nothing wrong with him and that it was the world around us that was crazy.

That night, I wrote in bed by candlelight.

Dear Dad, I love you so much. I'm scared to talk to you about this. But I found your records, from when you were in Chillicothe, Mom sent them to me a long time ago. Dad, you were sick. You should have taken the medication. When you stopped, you became a monster, I was terrified to be around you. But I loved you, Dad, and you treated me horribly. You taught me to feel crazy. All I ever did as a little girl was wipe away your tears. It wasn't everybody else who was crazy, Dad. You have problems, you had a chance to get help, for me, Dad. You could have done it for me. Until you are willing to say you are sorry for the things you did, I will not have contact with you.

The next morning I folded the letter; its notepaper lines stained with tears, its white spiral margins tangled in the chaos of one another, refusing to separate.

I expected Dad to call me when he got it. He might be mad for a while but we would work it out on the phone. He would say he was sorry he hurt me and that yes, he knew that he saw things differently and had paranoid thoughts. He was sorry he didn't take the medication they gave him. He wishes he had done better. In that small conversation, all would be forgiven. We would be laughing by the time we got off the phone and the rest of our life together would be from a new place, a new start, with the love a dad and his daughter can have.

A week went by and no Dad. I pick up the phone and call him.

"Dad? Did you get my letter?" I choke out.

"Fuck you, bitch." He growled and hung up.

I called the V.A. hospital and tracked down the man who wrote the most damning page of my father's report. Partly retired and practising in a small town a few hours away, I made an appointment as a new client and drove to see him.

I walked into his office and slapped the page down with his name at the top, the same one he'd typed when he suspected I might be being held as a hostage by my father. I slapped down a school photo as a girl, the same age I was when my father descended into madness.

"You wrote this record. This is me when I was sixteen. I was held as a hostage by my father in the trailer. You knew about me and you didn't do a damn thing. You had a moral obligation as a doctor to report it if you thought I was being abused. Why didn't you help me?"

The old psychiatrist looked down over the rims of his glasses, shuffled the paperwork around. "Well, my dear," he drawled slowly. "I'm sorry for what happened to you, but you see, I was hired only as an independent contractor. It was my job to interview your father, just as other doctors did, and write this report. The reports go to an unidentified third party for review before they release the patient. There really isn't anything I could have done. Sad to say, these records probably didn't make it to anyone that decided to release your father. They just stayed in his file in case anyone checked. It's quite an unfortunate part of the system."

I took my pent-up rage to that doctor. I wanted to make him pay, for turning me against my dad, for sending him home, for not making sure Dad took the drugs. The old man's words rang empty as he blathered about who wasn't responsible for anything. As I stared at him, I saw another layer of the truth. He just didn't care. In his work, he sees thousands of fucked-up people. I was just another kid who fell through the cracks. I walked out of his office and flatlined. It was all I could do to drive home.

I tried to talk to my brother but it just reopened an angry wound.

"What do you expect, Sis? You really hurt my father with that letter." Danny, laying single claim to Dad as if I've been disowned. "All that shit happened a long time ago. Let it go."

"But I can't have a real relationship with Dad if he won't even say he's sorry for what he did. It's not like I'm asking for much."

"Why does he have to? If you really loved him, you would never bring it up with him."

And in one fell swoop, both the father and brother I loved so much fell away from me. The holidays came and no one called. Even a crappy Christmas playing Santa Claus to them was quarantined off from me.

In the wake of a punishing silence, I gave, sold or burned the rest of my possessions and headed west to California in a blizzard just before the New Year. I wanted my father to protect me from Mom. I wanted him to protect me from himself. I wanted the brother I'd do anything for to make a stand for me. I thought if it came down to losing me as their sister or daughter, that someone would apologize for something. But drawing a hard line left me alone and ostracized. What happened in my childhood was my rightful duty as Dad's keeper. I was the throw-away girl, the resident family photo taker, the all-occasion present-buyer who should never ask for anything in return.

I drove out in the blizzard without telling a soul. I told myself I'd just go find a new family, people who could care about me. But the people I met couldn't hold a candle to the omnipotence I felt with my father or the closeness I once had with Danny.

But still, I hold out hope for something to bring us back together. Danny calls from the garage apartment he shares with Dad and whispers that they'll be coming through California, hauling cars. He'd work on Dad on the way, he said, maybe we could all meet then. I wait each day, anxious for the call from my brother to say he and Dad are close. He calls from a payphone and tells me that Dad still doesn't want to see me, not after what I've done.

"But, Danny," I whine. "It's been years."

"Sis," Danny whispers. "If Dad even knows I'm talking to you, I'll be in big trouble. I might have to hang up here soon if he walks over."

It takes a minute to realize Danny has hung up on me. I click the phone down and cry in the tub. I've been on my own for so long, I can't even remember what it's like to have family.

Chapter Ten

I have not seen my father in seven years. After they shunned me in California, I moved to England with a boyfriend and travelled on the fly with him whenever I could. And I have only just recently come back to Ohio, to revisit the site where I'm writing a book about growing up in Ohio and more specifically, about the things that happened to me at my mother's hand.

Dad, Danny and I are gathered here today by the torn ligament in my brother's knee. I have seen Danny once or twice since I've been back, but I haven't spoken to my father.

Dad drove Danny to the medical centre, I will drive him home. His surgery will take a few hours and my father and I will be stuck in a waiting room together, hashing it out in silence or violence. I am terrified he'll be in the same place where he left me; his last spitting words to me seared in my mind. My heart has lived quietly sheltered by a briar patch all this time: the same thorns that protect me from his rejection pierce me too.

I spot them in the waiting room; my heart races.

"Hey, Sissy." Dad breaks the silence. "Good to see you."

We file into Danny's prep room and flank his hospital bed, each of us talking to him as if the other weren't standing right there.

When they wheel my brother away, my father asks if I'll have breakfast with him in the cafeteria, up on the second floor. I take the steps, he rides in the elevator. My father has grown, tipping the scale at 300 pounds. I cannot imagine squeezing into a box with him.

We set our trays down and my father opens his mouth, closes it, opens it again, gasping like a guppy, trying to find the words. He snakes his hand across the table and covers my own, lying face down on the fake veneer wood.

"Sissy," he starts. My eyes stare empty across the table.

"You, me, Danny, we been through a lot. There's been a lot of bad times. But I want you to know that the only thing I got out of my nineteen years of hell married to your mother," he chokes up, "is my two beautiful kids."

He squeezes my hand. My eyes shift from the space in front of me down to my Styrofoam plate of scrambled eggs.

"You're my baby. You were always my baby." Dad cries.

In his broken words, my heart makes a subtle shift to the light, rising to the shine like a rose to sudden sun. I thaw just a crack to receive what was lost a long time ago, my father. Our seven-year gap begins to close in an instant, like the old days when he could make it up to me with just a shared egg roll.

"I love you, baby," he says in the siren song to call me back.

I squeeze his hand. "I love you, too."

He leans in close, as if to share a secret. "Listen, it don't matter to me that you was a prostitute, or that you smoked crack and hung out with niggers doing drugs."

My hand goes limp.

"You're my baby and I love you. I can accept you now for who you are."

The hum and burble of the aquarium calms me. I focus on the fish, look at the clock; it isn't a cuckoo clock but it might as well be. We have another two hours before it's time to go.

* * *

Dad helps Danny hobble into my car in the parking lot. While I stand behind them, I spot a man taking his baby daughter out of the car seat, lifting her so gently, so lovingly and pressing her in strong arms to his chest. He would never let her fall. I wonder if my dad could have been trusted with me as a baby like this. I wonder if he would have forgotten me in the back seat or on the roof of the car or just plopped me next to him while he drove instead of taking the time to buckle me in.

Something shatters inside me right there in the parking lot. My father hadn't changed. I had. I had been looking to him through the eyes of a little girl, trusting and sure that he would love and protect me as his child. But just as my father couldn't see me, I couldn't see him. I wasn't ever going to get the father I wanted or needed. I had this one, this gross, boisterous, belching, farting, disgusting wild man who said he loved me like crazy, even if I was a crack whore.

I decide to use my father and our relationship to study myself, to alter the formula that keeps me attracting men like him. I am now in my early thirties, I am a professional of sorts, speaking to groups and college classes about child abuse, as well as writing my own childhood memoir. But inside, at the centre of my being, I am still a girl, a seventeen-year-old looking for innocent love with a boy my age who is also stunted in his emotional maturity. The beginnings are always the same, fun dates of dancing to Eighties music and sleeping outside under the stars, watching cartoons and basically being the kids we were never allowed to be. But little by little, my boyfriends turn from child-like boys into paranoid men. If I come home with cool new couch pillows to excitedly show them, my boyfriend thinks I've had an orgy on the last ones and ransacks the house searching for stains on them. If I buy a piece of furniture, another boyfriend accuses me of giving the store clerk a hand job for it. I begin to offer intricate details of every place I go, in the hope that I can quell his paranoid thoughts before he has them. He checks the receipts and times when I get home and calls the store to see if someone remembers me being there. When I take too long in the bathroom of a store, my boyfriend thinks I've snuck a strange man in there with me. Nothing I do in my relationships with these men is taken at innocent face value. They are all searching for the complication, the trick, the wool being pulled over their eyes, the delicious feeling they will get to catch me in the act, betraying them with another. And I spend my days trying to prove my love, until all my convincing becomes unconvincing.

* * *

219

Since Dad's intimate chat with me over breakfast, he calls often. I decide to let him, and to use the interactions to glean clues for myself. Sitting in the parking lot of Target, I grab the phone.

"Hey, Dad."

"Hey, Sissy, got a minute? You know, I was just thinking, there might be something to that book you wrote, to your mother hurting you."

Duh. I let him continue.

"Do you remember when your shoulder came out of socket?"

"I first broke my arm in second grade, are you talking about that?"

"No, this musta been when you was around two."

"No, Dad," I say tired, "I don't remember anything from being two."

"Well, Sandy said you fell off the couch and your shoulder came out of socket. The doctor pulled me aside, asked me if I seen it happen. I said no, but you know, she's my wife, I backed her up. Well, he took me aside and said he thought she did it, said your arm didn't fall out, it got pulled out."

And just like that, my father sucks me back into the family drama, to all the pain of my childhood.

"You know, Sissy, I never thought nothing of it until you wrote that book."

Sitting quietly in a Target parking lot, with one of my earliest moments of harm conveyed to me nonchalantly by the one person who could have protected me, the dam breaks. I drop the phone and slump against the steering wheel.

"I'm sorry, Sissy," I can hear my father say softly, "I'm real sorry I didn't help you."

My father's legs are as hairless as if they had been wiped clean with Nair. He is lugging his hulk of a hardened body up the concrete steps of my porch stoop and into my house. Halfway up he wavers a little, leaning back, the slow start of a daughter-crushing fall. I steady his back and push the bulk of his form forward, hoping to God I can offset his weight and he doesn't flatten me. He limps into the house. A little wheeze squeezes out with each exhale. My father is on the addictive painkiller Percocet for a back injury he sustained when the delicate ankles that support his 350-pound, pear-shaped body tripped over a crinkle in the rubber floor mat of a farm store. And true to the sue-age of American culture, he is in Columbus today trying to find a lawyer to sue for pain and suffering. He takes two painkillers every four hours, then he slips and says sometimes he takes two every two hours. He thinks this was a two-hour time. He can't remember.

* * *

My dog is happy, joyously happy to see people at my home. He's like a Martha Stewart host. He greets them at the door, smiling widely; he might as well be standing on two legs, wearing an apron and holding a tray of fresh-baked cookies. My father plops onto the couch. The dog, a regal white English setter, leaps in one graceful bound to my father's side, attentive. He talks to the dog about going to the library. The dog licks the corner of his mouth, a paw lain upon my father's heaving, exasperated chest.

"Yor such a pweety dog, yes you are! Yes you are!"

And there he is, my father, baby talking to the dog with an affection never shown to us. Then he turns back into the man I know.

"So the nigger at the Arthur Treacher's gave 'em a cup of water."

He is telling my dog a story about his dog, Floyd. Not to be confused with his cat, who he calls Pink.

"So anyway," he continues, the dog listening intently. "Listen, now, you're not listening to me. We gave Carol the cup of watta and Floyd slopped it all over her." He is slipping into a Percocet nod. "I'm lewsing my phone loll the goddamn time, I sitz on the couch and the couth eats it, then I have to have the goddamn boy acrozz the street come over and fish my phone out of the goddamn couch."

I sit across the living room from him and listen along with the dog. He has been in my house for fifteen minutes and not looked at me once.

My father drifts asleep, his head flops back along the top of the couch, hanging like a fat melon on the vine off his neck, depressing a gully along the top of the cushions. His mouth hangs open, catching flies, both his arms lain out at his sides, palms open. I sit and watch him, while the dog, having lost his audience, gives a sigh and slumps his chin in my father's lap.

I adopted the dog the same week I terminated my pregnancy. I did not mean to get pregnant. But there in the bathroom, a week earlier, I held a positive strip in my hand and caught my grief-stricken face in the mirror. I had gained the courage to leave a violent, paranoid boyfriend only two weeks earlier and couldn't believe how stupid I was to end up pregnant. He didn't start off violent and paranoid, he started off funny, unpredictable, childlike and with the delicate vulnerability and frustrated tears that had once bound me to my father. But I would wake to him sniffing my hair like the velociraptor in *Jurassic Park*, leaning inches from my face and sneering that I smelled of another man. I was scared – of him and of myself for not leaving. Why couldn't I just get up on my own two legs and walk out the door? But my body lay comatose on a mattress stripped bare, in the dead of winter with only a filthy sheet to cover me. Night after night, I curled beside him, eyes wide open, pressing my frozen fingertips into one of his many warm crevices as he soundly slept; a balmy armpit, the crook of a knee, anything to draw the heat of him into my cold body. And I could not find my way out his door and to my own warm apartment. There was a part of my brain that was screaming at me to get up and leave, to break the spell but I lay in a stupor, like Nancy on the bed she shared with Sid as the room blazed around her.

To bear a baby by this man meant to go it alone without any support and live with the knowledge in the back of my mind that at any time he could reel in legal rights to share the child. I could not subject a cell half the size of my pinky to that possibility, or commit myself to living with that fear for the rest of my life. He had stalked me, beaten down the door of my own apartment. He had threatened my life and curled up on the threshold of my door. The ultrasound dated conception at two weeks. It was our last time and he had hurt me. I might have walked away, but I was crippled. I did not trust myself to not go back if there was any reason to. And I know too well, a restraining order never stopped a bullet.

The clinic gave me three white pills to take home. It would feel like a heavy cycle they said. It would give me dignity in one of the most private choices a woman can make they said. I was to swallow two pills at once, then the last one a half hour later. I lit the fireplace in my small room and kneeled on the rug. One hand pressed to my belly, the other held the pills. I closed my eyes.

"Dear God, please. I am asking that this baby return to you. I cannot give her the protected life I promised. I cannot do it alone. I'm sick. And I can't choose men who aren't sick. Please guide her to the light of heaven. Please I beg you, let her return to me when I can give her a family of happiness."

I cried for this child, for the circumstances which had led me to this, for my stupidity. Asking her to return was as close as I could get to the promise that her every day would be free from abuse or neglect, that no one in her life would ever hold a biological right to treat her as my father did me, to hit her, confuse her, to attach to a father that made her scrape for every bit of love like a crumb from the carpet. My hand grew hot, pressed to my belly. I opened my other hand. It was 11 pm.

The first two pills I took standing in the kitchen at the counter, a glass of water in hand.

The cramps will be like a bad period.

By the time I took the next one, I was standing on the red rug in front of the fireplace, the pain buckling my knees and dropping me to the floor. The fire snapped and I lay paralysed, curled on my side in its glow. My limbs started kicking like a heroin addict, an arm flinging out, a leg jerking up, my eyes rolling back in my head.

I could have died. I could not crawl to the phone. I lay there, my arms and legs flinging wildly. I screamed in pain, no one heard, or if they did, they chose not to help. Hours passed and only my eyes could see the clock on the mantle. 1 am. 2 am. 2:30 am. I watched my body as if cut off from it. Six hours later, I slept.

When I woke, it was morning. Bruised and disorientated, I drove to the pound and adopted the emaciated white English setter. He was covered in piss, hunkered in the back of his cage, shaking like a leaf.

This is the dog that smiled on my father as he hobbled into my house today. This is the dog that lay his head in his lap.

In my favourite red chair, across from my snoring father, it dawns on me that all the men are of my bad choice, and within them is the key to Dad and the stunted, shrivelled place inside me. A place I have to run back to and grab the girl I left behind, then get the hell out. And it is in these men, with their little-boy charm, tears and paranoia that I search for the father to save, to serve, to win protection of, to beg protection from. There in my red chair, I see the shriveled-up part of me lying on the rug like a dried-up prune, the driving force behind an insanity that defies all of my intelligence, class and grace. In my red chair, I devise a plan to beat the odds. I'll do it again; if I can just get the answer, maybe I can change the question.

"I had a dream about my mother the night she died," Dad recalls when he wakes up groggy on the couch. "She stood at the foot of my bed, wanted to make sure she got me raised, she said everything was going to be fine. I sat up and told your mother about it, she told me I was crazy. Later that night I got a call from her doctor, he called me to say Mom passed away. She had high blood pressure, diabetes, water around her heart. She was only 42.

"I went down to the hospital and there was my father, shaking my mother's dead body, 'C'mon Annie, wake up.' He was drunk, didn't even realize she was dead." Dad pauses. "Ten years later. Friday before Mother's Day, in the V.A. hospital in Dayton, Ohio, he called me, sounded like he was drunk, he was crying how much he missed Annie. I got a call from the V.A. not an hour later, told me he died. I said, doc, that can't be true, I just talked to him on the phone.

Doc said he had no idea why he died, they couldn't find a thing wrong with him."

My dad gets teary eyed, "I can tell you why he died." A single tear forms to hang on his bottom lid. "He died of loneliness."

The tear splashes down his cheek like a stone skipped. He's not crying for the father he lost, he's crying for the life he never had with him.

Chapter Eleven

At 6 A.M. my father drove his truck off the side of a mountain in rural Georgia. It was a thirty-foot drop and they all went careening over the side; the dully truck, the loaded car trailer, the 15-year-old shop hand he'd dubbed Goober Jr.

When they finally cu-clunked to a stop at the bottom of the mountain gully, the engine was on fire and my father's massive belly was wedged behind the steering wheel, his teeth knocked loose from the impact against it.

He calls me from the payphone in the lobby of a medical centre.

"Sissy, you got to help me," he labours. "I'm in so much pain, feels like I got a broken back."

I offer to drive down there and help. I talk to the hospital. They've already X-rayed and released him. The pain is arthritis from his previous back injury and, they say, he has no broken bones.

Dad has his shop boy drive them back to Ohio in a rented car and my father, lodged fast into the front seat of a compact car, pops Percocets like they're M&Ms.

When they arrive home, he ends up in the emergency room of a local hospital, screaming in pain, swearing his back is broken. They check him in and rush a morphine drip into his arm.

I live the closest to the hospital now so I'm the first to arrive. Instead of finding my father in medical peril, I find him enthralled with an audience of fussing nurses hustling in and out of his curtained cubicle.

"Heeey, Sissy," he shouts out in party order. "I was just telling nurse Debbie here the story." He is animated, soaring, while the nurse fiddles with his morphine line.

"The South is a different world Debbie, see, it hasn't changed much since the Confederate days." He licks his lips, indicating an oncoming story. "So I drove the truck off at dawn, right – swerved to miss hitting a deer, last one cost me a fucking grill on the truck and I fall, oh I don't know, twenty thirty feet in the gully off the mountain." My father drops his jaw, pantomiming the drama. "I couldn't get out of the truck! The sheriff comes, says," he slips into sheriff mode, 'Can you climb up out of this embankment boy?' I said, 'No, officer.' Them sums-a-bitches stood up there on the rim and laughed. 'Well scramble up out of there like a pig, we can't get down there and get you, boy.' That's what the sheriff told me." He adds another jaw drop for effect. "I couldn't even move, my teeth all rattling around in my head. I was drooling blood. When the ambulance came they lowered down a wire basket. They winched me up the side of that mountain like a hog in a shopping cart."

My father is over 300 pounds. This is not difficult to imagine.

My brother arrives, swept up in worry, glossy with tears. "Hey, Buddy." He grabs my father's toes under the sheet and shakes.

Dad bellows, his fingers claw out for the bedrail and clench around it in pain. It's the first sign of how much he hurts. But he's high as a kite and it only takes a few minutes for the narcotic to wash over him.

"So they get me up the mountain, fuckers took me to a medical centre down there, right? To get me some X-rays. When I'm at the hospital, I tell the nigger pushing the wheelchair, I said, 'My back is killing me,

I'm in pain here.' He's pushing me down the hall, the chairs going thump ta thump ta thump," my dad rolls his eyes, "I look down, see why I'm getting jostled around, and he's fucking got me in a wheelchair with a flat tyre."

My brother laughs.

"The South," Dad croons, "No boy, you stay away from the South. They'll get you down there."

Alive with plans, he assigns duties. "Okay, look now, so all we need to do is find someone who has a crew cab dully truck and a hitch and we can pay them to haul the rental car back down to Georgia on Monday, then they can haul my truck back up here. Who do we know Goober that has a crew cab dully we can send down there?"

Danny and I look at each other. Danny laughs, "I think, buddy, that this is the last thing you need to be worrying about right now." He pats Dad's leg higher up under the sheet.

Dad scans our faces with shining eyes and a big dopey smile. "What, you don't think your old man is cool? I'm so cool I came out with sunglasses on. You don't think I can't get outta here by Monday? I'm going home this weekend, ain't I Nurse Debbie? They just gotta figure out where this fucking pain is coming from." And he pumps his thumb on the little self-medicating button on his morphine drip.

Nobody knew how many Percocets he popped before he got there so the hospital treated him as if he was clean.

Just after midnight, my father OD'd.

The tears you cry for your father are different to the tears you cry for yourself. An absolute surrender to loss, there is no suicidal thought involved, no escape hatch or self-absorbed overdose you line up. It's just the opposite. You'd do anything to be there, to see him come back, to have his turnaround hinge on the words you whispered, the lists of things you say you'll do together when he gets out, the agreements you make with God, the power of your love, the sheer indomitable strength of will alone. What once was the duty of seeing him for his birthday becomes suddenly, in the moment of loss, a desperate longing to have just one more. Where I had cut my father's visits down to as few and far between as possible, I was now unable to leave his side.

He survived the drug overdose, but now lay in a coma.

Gone is my father; vibrant, glassy-eyed, shouting out in good cheer, making some nurses laugh and others cringe crimson in embarrassment. The Benny Hill of Ohio, he is now hooked to a ventilator, tied to the bed, in a neck brace and a back brace, with a cornucopia of machines fanned out around the bed breathing for him. A tube is white-taped to his nose, snot cakes around the plastic. The doctors think his back is broken although they can't wheel him to X-ray to know for certain until he stabilizes. But a broken back is the least of his worries. His overdose sent him into cardiac arrest and his Agent Orange lungs operate at the permanent capacity of full-blown pneumonia. So it is the respirator that forces his lungs open and shut to intake enough oxygen. And because waking to a machine that breathes for you is one of the most frightening experiences a person can come around to, his hands are tied to the bedrails to prevent him from pulling out the breathing tube – or any of the other tubes stuck in him.

My father, his life hangs in the balance between life and death.

My brother and I sit in the critical-care waiting room. My brother balls up his fists, trying to hold it in. I sit next to him, quietly weeping. Dad was fine yesterday, whooping it up with the nurses, saying he was going to be home by Monday. I didn't know it could work like this, no one did. An audible sob leaks from my brother and I turn to hold him. We are not crying for losing the life we had with our father, we are crying for the life we never had.

* * *

Dad's ventilator goes off like the ooga ogga horn of Mr T or the bullhorn he used to bellow through at the football games when I shrunk in humiliation.

Holding vigil in his dark room, I remember the things I did as a little girl that my dad thought were funny or handled with the grace of a moderate parent, allowing me to make mistakes, allowing me to be the child. Learning all the words to *American Pie;* my dad's record collection; finding the Chubby Checker collectible album and peeling off all the stickers. My father could have roared, he could have whipped off his belt, or slapped my hand. His records were all he had as Mom's possessions exploded to fill every crack and crevice of the trailer. But all he did was suck in his breath and say with a steady quiver, *We can't do that to any more of Daddy's albums, okay?*

When I could not spell a word, he spelled it out for me. He played eye spy on long car rides and when Mom ducked into a gas station to buy a pack of cigarettes, he'd ask me "how do you spell cigarette, Sissy?" And told me how bad they were, making me promise him that I'd never smoke. He'd tell me how smart I was when I knew a '67 Pontiac from a '68 just by looking at the fender. In the absence of certainty about my father's survival, it is not that all the terrible things he did go forgotten, but that the tiniest details of his efforts are suddenly magnified.

Ding, ding

The systemic soft ding of a machine alarm goes off somewhere on the floor from one of the hushed rooms.

Ding, ding.

Another one goes off, exact in its steady warning. The soft bells have an underlying urgency in their ring; they mean something; a machine gone haywire, a life slipping. The other bell dings in the distance and they alter in tandem. They sound like the upscale chimes heard in fine department stores. But I now they're not.

My dad, the giant Fabergé egg; a colossal hamster with a broken back. Leathery skin, swollen wrists, his hair grazed to fuzz, beads of condensation dangle from his moustache like dewdrops from dainty woodland foliage.

I lean over his bed and smooth a cool washcloth over his sweaty forehead. His breath is sour, his tongue swollen, his lips cracked. A tube crusted with blood snakes down his throat. I wish I could wash away his pain. I do what I can; smear balm on his lips, gently wash his face with aromatic soap made from crushed pine needles, bring in freshly crisped bacon and waft it under his nose.

Outside his window, the sky is smooth as corn silk, blue as baby power.

The heat of my hand smoothes my father's forehead, I use my palm as an iron, pressing slowly over his scalp, melting wrinkles from his face.

With my father in a coma and a part of his brain unplugged, I feel close to him, finally at peace being next to him. I don't feel like I have a wild chimpanzee on my hip, who at any given moment will poop, pick his nose or leap from my shoulder to swing on the chandelier.

The weeks tick by. I hate being here; the fat Ohioans waddle slowly down the hospital corridors, my lean muscular legs strike long strides past them, burning rubber down the hall. In the summer heat, their flip-flops swish swivel hips lazily through the hospital in a slow saunter. They don't deserve to be here. Although I wish them no harm, I wish them gone. This place is only for the most important situations and anyone with an amble like that better get the fuck out of my way. At the entrance to the hospital are several signs printed with the image of a gun in a red circle, a slash running through it, reminding people not to bring their loaded weapon into the hospital. In light of the morons seen wandering through here, the sign seems well placed.

Day after day, we wait. I spend soap opera hours with my father; Danny comes for the sitcom set. I feel guilty for not wanting to be here. My brother holds rage in his clamped jaw, Dad's comeback the only thing he can't control in his life. I reserve my own anger for the fat, Midwestern cows that congeal in the waiting rooms, grazing from the snack machines. They cram into the elevator on my way up to Dad's room, bubbly and excited that a relative's in the hospital, oozing a drama into the air that something tragic could happen; exchanging details of procedures and the percentage poor Uncle Eddie has of making it.

The ventilator wheezes in and out. I hold my father's hand, smooth my thumb in the deep groove of his severed artery.

A long, long time ago.

I lean in close, whisper-sing

And I can still remember how that music used to make me smile.

And I knew if I had the chance that I could make those people dance and maybe they'd be happy for awhile.

On my day shift at the hospital, I look through my brother's stack of pictures, amazed. Photos of Dad with his truck and trailer, three, four cars or vans piled up onto the rafters, pictures of Dad with wild man hair, streaks of grease, lying on the pavement, his mound of belly wedged under the frame, arms extended up into the gut of the engine, wrench in hand, trying to fix a problem and creating a new one. I feel privy to a side of their life I've never known before, one I can never share with my dad no matter how hard I try, one that is a son's dream, building cars with his vintage-obsessed father. I gaze at stacks of Polaroids taken of them smiling in the shining sun with local race car celebrities, shaking hands, beaming for the camera, natural smiles, the smiles of men, men who inhabit an entire existence without women. I wonder if I could have a life without men. I cannot go one day without thinking of a boyfriend, and I cannot think of a single place I would want to go without them with me.

Up until now, my brother and I have had our father to ourselves, trading shifts during the week and both arriving on the weekends to share time in the room. One Saturday the room is electric with tension. My father's longtime partner, Carol, occupies the only chair, my brother stands at my father's bed, scowling. Buried in a romance novel from the library, Carol has brought a medical contraption with her and the room whirs with the sound of it. Clamped around her foot is a small inflated tent filled with dry ice, having had a few toes recently amputated because of diabetes-related gangrene.

"What's wrong, Danny?" I whisper to him.

"Nothing," he snaps.

"Danny's just not used to being around death, Julie," Carole says, never looking up. "I am. I've been around dead people my whole life. You just have to accept that your father is going to die sometime."

My brother glares.

"He's not dead yet," Danny growls, "Don't talk about my father like that." He catches his hands squeezing Dad, "Oh geez, Dad, I'm sorry." He looks like he's about to cry. "I shouldn't have said that, you're not going to die, I'm here, Sis and me are going to stay right here, we'll get you better."

We are not telling our mother; it will be about a lawsuit, a funeral, a Krovorkian proposed mercy death wish just so she can get a peek at the will. She will not miss a beat in asking about the details to calculate a return. In this perfect triad, me, Danny, Dad, there is no trace of the Gregory clan. Our life now together, even if only for this moment, feels sacred.

I talk to Danny about getting power of attorney for Dad so that if any important decisions did need to be made, we would be in control of them, not Mom or Carol. I ruminate about D&J GTO and how so long ago we had such big plans for a family business with the three of us. Danny stops me cold and looks at me like I'm crazy.

"The J doesn't stand for Julie, Sis. The D&J stands for Daniel Joseph. That's my middle name."

My brother seeks comfort from anyone in a white lab coat. Although they can tell him nothing new, his engineer's mind craves the science of percentages and numbers, cold hard facts he can cling onto in a time when anything goes. I crumble in my own quiet way. I know my father can die and, even if I occupy myself with scurrying around caring for his comatose body, I cannot escape that reality. Seeing Danny when I come in the room brings it all home. My father's anguish, etched onto the lines in my brother's face, awash with worry. Where he can show it but not feel it, I feel it even more deeply, for the both of us. My brother has the same brand of delusional optimism that shields him from the brutal truth about our mother; believing what he needs to believe, that she is a perfectly good person and not the one who pitted us against our father. And so too, he refuses to acknowledge that Dad might not make it. I know my father might die at any time and in the silence of his room, I make my peace by telling him everything I need to say. And I sing; lines from our favourite songs that seem written for this time. I hold his hand, brushing my fingers softly down his,

You're so far away, doesn't anybody stay in one place anymore?

It would be so fine to see your face at my door.

And it doesn't help to know you're so far away.

Everybody wants a slice of him. Danny clings to his illusion, Carol is talking death and I walk the tightwire between them both; willing Dad to live, knowing he could die.

Day 21. Come on, Dad. Show me a sign. I graze the peach fuzz of my father's head. If I was a child, I would fling my arms around him. The mini CD player is on, the TV finally off, Simon and Garfunkel's *Bridge Over Troubled Water* plays on a loop.

See how they shine. If you need a friend.

Like a bridge over troubled water, I will lay me down.

Like a bridge over troubled water. I will ease your mind.

I sing to Dad as I organize the room,

Home, where my thoughts escaping

Home, where my music's playing

Home, where my love lies waiting, silently for me.

C'mon Dad, let's go home.

And here's to you, Mrs Robinson

Jesus loves you more than you will know.

And suddenly, in the rapid beat, the tip of my father's finger starts to tap in perfect time to the music, *whoa, whoa, whoa*.

My dad opens his eyes, shock, fear, and closes them again.

I run for the nurse. She toddles in, toddles out.

I call my brother, ecstatic with good news.

I think of my dad growing cantaloupes and selling them by the bushel on the base with me swinging my legs on the tailgate of the station wagon, the night summer air ripe with sweet melon. His goofy ass, happy-go-lucky grin, hanging out with Rolly Polonka and Tommy Templeton, his old buddies from the Air Force base. I think about my father's light way about life. If my dad had not have lived in such a starving life, I wonder if he would have ever found himself on that Sherex rooftop to begin with – or any of the other places he went when I was a kid. Without Mom's noose around his neck, my father is a beloved man, not as in a good man, but in the way a larger-than-life boisterous personality is. You can't sit down and talk serious with him, he won't be much comfort at a funeral, but he'll make you laugh, he'll fart out loud and cackle like a little boy, cracking jokes at the most tender of things. He'll talk back to the TV like it's a real debate and make everybody out to be stupid, rolling his eyes in mock disbelief at the insanity of the world and everyone in it. And in this way, he is more real than most; he won't insult you behind your back; he'll do it straight to your face.

The last time he was in the Chillicothe mental hospital, he said to his roommate, "Let me introduce you to my baby, my daughter." He called me his angel. I wanted to feel a swell of pride, of love, of belief. But I felt nothing – only that I was privy to the unwitting sham of making it seem as if we were close. I was too old by then to buy into the hope of it.

And here in the hospital, that time melts away. Maybe my father isn't a good man, maybe he didn't know how to protect me or love me as I thought a real dad should. But there is intrinsic value to his being; he may not give to people, but is just a tsunami life force, a joy to behold for those who don't need him like I did, always an uncertainty as to what expletives will flow or rapid-fire shoot from his mouth and at least this guarantees one an adventure – for better or worse.

But when I was just a small girl, I remember this about my father; getting home late in the dark, I'd pretend to be asleep in the back seat so Dad would scoop me up and carry me in. I snuggled into his chest, hiding my smile in its shadows.

"Boy," my father played along, "She sure is fast asleep, she's not gonna wake up for anything, not even if I tickle her."

And he's got me. I cannot suppress a giggle. Just trying to makes me laugh. It is a game we play, me and Dad, over and over without tiring.

My mother barks, "Julie. Wake up. We know you're not asleep."

But Dad has me halfway down the gravel walkway toward the house.

I realized that Mom had derailed my life with him; that he had loved me, but she was so threatened by what he gave his daughter that she came to play on his paranoia – making me testify against him on the stand and making up names she said I called him behind his back. Lies that undermined an already fragile trust between us until the bond broke, like the dry and splintered wishbone of Christmas past. And here in the hospital, with her thousands of miles away, she cannot touch us. The child in me returns, it comes out and is close with my father. Sitting perfectly still by his side, my father lifts my hand, slowly draws it to his face and kisses it in slow motion. A tear slides down the side of his face, wetting the white pillowcase. I have not held my father's hand like this since I was a girl of seven, walking with him through the aisles of 7–11.

My father's been returned to me through the door-way of ICU.

He is awake now, with deep weathered lines in his face and sunken eyes.

"That you, God?" he calls out.

His male nurse sweeps into the dark room and tries to orient him to time, person, place.

"Dan, what your daughter's name?"

"Jewelly."

"Dan, what your son's name?"

Silence. He can't remember.

Danny walks in, solid as granite. "Hey buddy, what's going on, looking good, looking good, glad to see you."

I can only cry, take my father's hand. Coming out of the coma, his eyes strain to open, it's still a labour to live. Even though he's awake, he's not out of the woods. He still needs the respirator and ventilator to breathe as his lungs are too weak to keep him alive. They're fairly certain his back is broken but they cannot move him to X-ray without risk of paralysing his spine.

The purple and green diamond gown looks ridiculous sprawled across his mammoth frame; three hundred and thirty pounds of white human flesh. The furrows on his brow lie in thick folds. Just as I did 20 years ago, when I was in the hospital as a little girl, I reach my hand forward to touch my father's forehead. This time I make contact.

As part of my daily routine, I soak a washcloth in cool water and wring it out, wiping broad strokes over his face. I put on a favourite CD and rub my father's feet with peppermint lotion. He raises his fingers to whisp underwater charades, his hand moves heavy like the addict's nod. I come up to his bedside. When I slip my hand into his, my father's visibly quakes and lets out a sob for the love of me. In all my years of making him perfect toast, I was never this appreciated.

When my brother arrives for the night shift, I am still sitting with Dad in the dark, holding his hand. He taps his finger and slurs out to Danny, *Your sister paints pictures with words*.

My father has turned into a compulsive finger tapper. With a breathing tube snaked down his throat, his keeps a hand close to his chest and taps on it for everything. Rapid taps mean agitation, slow taps mean contentment, a single tap serves as an exclamation point. I sit by his side and cry. He does not know what to do with my tears. Nobody knows what to do with my tears. He taps his finger on his chest, restless.

My father gets shots in his belly every day. They stick needles in his stomach and he lies with bruised pockmarks like the remains of leeches suckered from his skin. He gets a searing flush chaser to his liquid narcotics in the IV, and his face contorts in pain. I tell him to squeeze my hand when it hurts, and he digs his nails into me, breaking skin.

The nurses finally leave. My father coughs, grimacing.

"Dad, can I get you anything?"

He forms an imaginary gun and puts it to his temple, *prow, prow*, he clicks the revolver. His eyes roll back. I cry for my father's pain.

"Dan," the nurse talks to him loud as if he's deaf, "It's Barbara." Or mentally slow, "I'm here to get you down to a CAT scan."

He rolls his eyes at her. He hates it. And if he wasn't on his last leg, the string of obscenities and insults he'd spew would knock her back a few feet.

I paint with words, lined up inside me. I can sometimes brushstroke the things I sense, the essence of a person or an experience, into a picture and transfer the feeling to the page. And that's when it hits me, what I share with my father: We are both storytellers, he is colourful in his oral renditions of events; I am rich with vivid description in writing. Both paint pictures for people that take them someplace, both make us beloved to a select few even though we are rough around the edges. It's not me that is special; it's the story that rushes out of me that is my only gift, however humble. On paper, I'm colourful. In person, my personality is jagged and broken, I'm like a junk-yard dog that's been chained in the yard and kicked: I need so much love but I snarl when approached.

I have unearthed my childhood love for my father, brushed it off and brought it out to light. I see that Dad did the things he did as he careened through life with our mother. Beneath the brutality that came from knee-jerk triggers, my father is fragile, in psyche and emotion. People can work their good magic on him or their black magic; his behaviour will be influenced one way or the other. He cannot feel any deeper than he can breathe.

And on day 45 my father woke up confused and yanked the tube that kept him breathing out of his throat. Everything collapsed. Bells and whistles sounded off and a code blue went out through the hospital. Staff on hand rushed to jumpstart his body before his brain died. One sliced an "X" at the base of my father's throat for a breathing tube; another shoved the balloon back down his windpipe swollen shut. It saved his life. And in the delicate days to follow, I held my breath. Like the omnipotent child who felt she alone could stop the car from falling on her father, I want to believe he's better because I play the music, because I wash his forehead with the cedar soap, because I will it so, because he kissed my hand only yesterday, intricately lacing the edges of his slipping world into my living one.

Beautiful clouds move painfully slow through a flawless blue sky. My father lies in a new coma, induced by doctors to help him stay on the machines without panicking. Carol lounges in the chair, reading, my brother and I stand by our father. I tend to him as always with cool washcloths, beard trimmers, nice soap.

My brother and Carol banter mindlessly while visitors from the classic car club file in and out over the weekend. People say the craziest things in a desperate hospital situation. They laugh at things that have no humour, trying to muster up the lightness they would have in the outside world.

"The nurses are pretty," my brother says.

"They sure are lucky you can't talk," he jokes.

"She ain't a redhead, but she'll do," Carol adds.

"Good deal, buddy." More soft laughter.

It's like all conversation gets boiled down to fifth grade stumpy sentences to contrast the seriousness of the reality.

"I'm going home to see Floyder," Carol says.

"Floyder, floyder, floyder," she sings.

Baby talking to my father, it makes me want to puke.

I proceed as if I have no power whether things work out. Danny proceeds as if he has the power to make things all work out.

"You all right buddy? Yeah, you feeling better? You feeling better, aren't you bud? Yeah, I thought so." My brother talks out loud, infusing words, thoughts, feelings right into his blind hopes and projections.

I hold my father's hand, and pray. *Weebles wobble but they don't fall down.*

Chapter Twelve

"Cover up my feet, Sissy, feels like they're running off."
My father drifts in and out of reality, a side effect of being weaned off eight weeks of coma-inducing narcotics. He lies rotting on his back in the rehabilitation wing of the hospital, where the severely injured learn to sit upright again, take their first steps and feed themselves with a spoon. The X-ray's revealed a cracked pelvis and two hairline fractures in his back; the staff keep him in a brace that often wiggles up under his chin and they turn him like a burrito every so often, keeping his spine straight.

We babysit him, my brother and I, as he comes back down. The first night giant spiders shoot from the ceiling on silvery threads and land on him.

"Get 'em off me!" he flails, swatting at his head.

He skins a dog the next night with his bare hands. I walk in the room as he lies sobbing, begging me to put the burning dog at the foot of his bed out of its misery. The next night he screams at the top of his lungs, that the staff are trying to kill him, waiting for him to fall asleep so they can hurl him out the seven-storey window – never mind he's still 300 pounds. The on-call doctor can't be reached to approve a sedative and Danny must turn around and drive the hour back to help him through the night. In all his weeks of surviving the real threat of death, it is his mind now that creates a visceral one.

I'm still on day watch, but with a gnawing feeling that my father slips from my grasp. He is awake now and I do not know what to say to him. With a trachea tube jammed in his windpipe, he can't talk much.

My father stares at the television, I read a magazine. We occupy the same space but are alone, like much of our life together. Pressed against the pages of a *People*, I catch the eye of a fashion model. The staged super-ficiality of the photo glares against the backdrop of my father's dependency, with his golden catheter tube hanging out of his sea green gown and his skin pocked with ruby black bruises from the needles they shoot him with every day.

* * *

My brother has located the first GTO my father ever owned and bought it from the dealership where it sat on the lot amidst late model Chryslers and Chevy sedans. To my brother it is the Holy Grail, the first iconic clad brick in the foundation of his life with Dad. He would spit-shine it with his tongue if he had to. For the time being, it sits in my garage so Danny can drive it over to the hospital and Dad can see it from his window.

I tell Dad I'm taking good care of it in the garage.

"You're more important than that old car," he weeps, "I don't know why I'm crying."

I walk around the corner to the wing where he is. Outside his room is a clear trash bag. It contains bed pads soaked with piss and the bag is smeared from the inside the colour brown. It has to be humiliating. A team of nurses attend my father inside the room; they stand around his bed, talk about him as if he isn't there and leave him exposed while they figure out their next step in moving his huge carcass and changing the soiled bed.

The end is in sight. In just a few more weeks, my father will be discharged from rehab and sent home, as soon as he can propel himself in a walker down the hall at least twenty feet by himself. The trachea tube has been removed and tape covers the gaping hole left in his throat. With each passing day, my father's mind and personality return with a vengeance to make up for lost time.

Propped on fluffed pillows in bed, he cradles the hospital room phone in the crook of his neck and calls the numbers in the little black book he's kept for years. He calls people he met ten years ago in Florida, remote relatives he hasn't spoken to in twenty years and a neighbour who lives down the street with her adult Down's syndrome son.

"Yeah, Shirley?" he scratches, with a tiny whistle from the hole in his windpipe, "Yeah, it's Dan. From down the street. How you doing, baby? Yeah, well listen, I was thinking about you and I'm worried that son of yours is going to push you down the basement steps and kill you. He's a big boy, Shirley, he could snap your neck if he wanted to. You ever think about that?"

And he's back. Wholly, specifically Dad. Glaringly, brazenly Dad.

The first time my father is able to sit up in a chair for longer than ten minutes, I'm the one to wheel him out the lobby for some fresh air. It takes a double wide wheelchair to accommodate his ass and three medical workers to load him into the seat of it. Once he's in, I'm on my own to push him.

"Look, Sissy, they said I lost 40 pounds on the coma diet. Isn't that great?"

"Fantastic, Dad." Two hundred and ninety pounds to my hundred and thirty.

I grab the rubber-coated handles and heave against the back of the chair as the wheels budge forward. Once in motion, it's just as difficult to slow down – whether for an elevator, a turn or another patient who appears on the horizon. I misjudge the trajectory of a corner and almost plough into someone, shuffling down the hall in their tube socks, pulling an IV pole along behind them.

"Jesus Christ," my father hisses, "You almost wrecked me, can't you even drive a fucking wheel-chair?" His voice is laced with animosity. He lets out one of his pressure-cooker release sighs. And I feel crushed, not just by his weight.

My father has no patience, with me, with other sick people, with the smokers on break just outside the doors, puffing in front of the "no gun" signs. Tired and wired, it's all he can do to sit for a few minutes at the edge of a circle of light streaming in the window before he's ready to go back to the room. I push him in silence, down the long hospital corridors, his harsh words still ringing in my ears.

* * *

The day we come to get him, my brother drives the red GTO he miraculously found and bought back. The series of events that shattered my life with Dad were fused back together by the coma and the unconscious loving man inside him; a glimpse of the fragile child still left that does not need to puff up in rage to protect itself or tarnish the potential intimacy of every moment with a belch or a fart or an inappropriate sex joke. That is the part of my father that I take with me this day, a part of him I always believed was in there, even if I forgot long ago what it felt like to be loved by him, even if I realize I have never known what it feels like to be protected by a father. For a brief shining moment, my father returned to me where I last left him, trapped in a hospital room, desperate for my help to get home. And for me, that's enough.

We wheel him out the hospital doors, the classic car gleams candy apple red in the late August sun. My father has made it. My brother poses with him, still in a wheelchair, by the hood of the car and I, the only girl, shrink back to my delegated role as the family photo taker.

Chapter Thirteen

At the restaurant, I help my father out of his truck. He has driven, against doctor's orders, up to Columbus to meet me for lunch, and the meal I promised if he made it; bacon-wrapped prawns. We sit at the table of his favourite Mexican restaurant; he visibly quakes from the pain. He rubs his forehead across an open palm, grimacing.

He sits across from me in the booth, picking his teeth with a toothpick, talking about our mother. "The woman was just a fucking nut, Julie. I don't know how I survived her."

He lets out a tightly coiled, wet belch. I turn my head, lean from the table. I agree our mother is a nutcase. But I don't know how the delicate child I was survived him either.

On the way out, my father swoops from sign to post to retaining wall, side-to-side monkey barring in the hopes he won't fall again. He is old school gruff, much like the guy on *American Choppers*. Only that guy still has his armour intact while my father's has broken. Everything his harshness once kept at bay leaks from him now. During every day, every interaction, he haemorrhages tears. The lion with an infected paw, the ogre old and decrepit, the bear mortally wounded. When I hug him goodbye, he tries to hold it in but he cries, shaking as his withered arms go up around me, stretched through the car window. It seems he cannot get near me, with my deep well of sadness, with my myopic awareness of the pain of the past and the severity of our family's dysfunction, without drinking from the well himself. Ten years later and my father's caught up with me. With my eyes holding steady the reflection of all that happened, he looks into them and cannot deny the pain. The gift of burden I carry as the family truth teller is a token he willingly takes from me now. Where once I saw his tears as coins to cleanse me, too much time has passed for me to have remained in that purgatory. Our family's poison held as a ruby in my throat for so long now, I see him cry, but it's me who is under glass. No longer with a child's heart, his tears fall on barren soul.

A week later, Dad is in his truck in my driveway, beaming, holding an industrial-sized pill bottle out the window. "Look at that, Sissy. I take thirty of these puppies a day, your druggie friends got nothing on me." His Percocets have been upgraded to OxyContin, one of the most powerful and addictive painkillers on the market.

"What'd you do to your chin, pop?" I examine a bloody gouge in his face.

"Oh, I cut myself shaving. That's what happens when you get old."

"I think it has more to do with you taking 30 painkillers a day then getting old."

My father's grin makes him look twelve. Despite a belligerence that churns beneath his skin and a well-honed ability to puncture on contact, he can still laugh at himself and exude boyish charm.

But part of it is the drug and I know it's just a matter of time before he crashes.

I write him a cheque for Christmas; the last thing he needs is another can of mixed nuts. I slide it through the window, 500 big ones, it's a lot for me to give but I want to help him with his backed-up bills and let him have some spending money. He did cheat death after all.

He folds it into his shirt pocket.

"Dad, look at it, it's for you, Merry Christmas."

He unfolds the cheque. "Well, thanks, Sissy," he humphs. "That won't even cover the parts I got at the junkyard."

In the town where my father lives, there's only one Ma and Pa gas station. In the parking lot is a vending machine that advertises: *Live Bait*. And as an afterthought, the company has added a warning on the front: *Not for human consumption*.

I am driving to my father's house after a frantic call. He didn't make it to the bathroom in time and shuffled through his own shit, tracking it through the house. He is crying, helpless and wants to die. He is alone with a hairline crack in his pelvis, with shit caked on the legs of his walker and a full blown addiction to painkillers. Carole is convalescing in a nursing home, the gangrene having eaten further up her foot. There is no housecleaning service for miles and I am armed today with $60.00 worth of cleaning supplies from the grocery store to tackle the mess.

The stench in my father's house is unbearable. The second it hits me, I throw my arm over my face and run outside to keep from puking. Shit, urine, sweat, b.o., rotten trash and the incontinent Floyd all rolled into one aromatic welcome wagon. I run out on the back porch and suck in my breath before racing back in to squirt cleaners on as much as I can.

My father's piss sits in an empty gallon milk jug, his version of a homemade non-invasive catheter. He lies beached in the La-Z-Boy, holding Pinky the cat. He mumbles sweet nothings in the dog's ear, which stretches out beside him on the sofa. Dad asks in a sheepish voice, "Sissy, would you fix me a piece of toast, with some marmalade. And would you bring me an O.J." Then a tone I've never heard before, "*Pleeease?*"

I smear margarine on with the back of a plastic spoon, thick pads of white scar the delicate top layer of toast. Then I lump some congealed marmalade and the crusty stuff from the rim on top. When you're little you want to make the best toast possible for your dad. When you're 35, you've caught on; don't encourage The King.

My throat closes from the fog of cleaning products that hang dense in the air. I'm allergic to everything. From the most desperate disparity beautiful things are forged. In my yellow industrial rubber gloves, on my hands and knees, I wonder:

Do borderlines ever get better?

Do narcissists ever see you?

Can you hold accountable the mentally impaired? Sure, in a court of law maybe but what about in the unspoken court of family?

Do the parents who never gave anything to their children ever stop taking from them?

Nursing homes are full of the elderly that no one comes to visit. The reason is easily framed as ungrateful adult children, selfishly wrapped up in their own lives, but little thought is given to any other context of why they aren't visiting. The parents who treated their kids like trash? They grow old, too. And their kids who came to see the truth, grow up as well. What's the correlation between children once beaten and the decrepit in nursing homes who once beat their children?

I look around at my father's white trash house. How does someone like me, born on the day of Liberace, come from something like this? How is my soul forged? Can I rise above?

These are my thoughts as I scrub the shit from my father's floor.

When Dad is back to driving, he picks me up at my house and we go out to lunch together.

Dad pulls into the intersection at a red light and turns left, cutting off the on-coming traffic.

"Pop, you just ran a red light."

"No I didn't, Sissy. I was in the intersection. I was committed."

"Okay, well just be careful."

My father thrusts his middle finger into the windshield, flipping off the driver as he barrels through the intersection. "Another fucking bitch, riding around, talking on the phone."

"Hmmm." I have started to wean myself from agreeing with everything he says.

"Yvette, she wanted to be gone in a hurry." He tells me the story again of how it was good riddance to lose her.

He can't grasp that he might have scared her by bringing his loaded gun to her nightstand with her kids in the house. He can't comprehend how this sweet woman, with her long grey hair and her hippie shop that sells tie-die T-shirts and Celtic leather journals and novelty pendants of goddesses and fairies wouldn't want his gun and matching paranoia in bed with her. He has taken the best thing he ever had and flipped it in his mind, making it about her worthlessness and framing her as a slut – just so he can survive the loss.

I don't think I've ever had a boyfriend that didn't do that too. *It's not my fault I lost my job. It's not my fault I didn't show for work. It's not my fault I got kicked out. It's not my fault I cheated.*

"Oh Jesus, what is that, a hooker?" Dad squints.

It's a girl in a tank top walking arm in arm with her boyfriend across the parking lot.

Dad hacks up a giant wad of gelatinous spit, rolls down his window and hawks it towards them.

Allow me to river dance. This is life with my father.

When Dad enters my house, my English setter greets him at the door. "What's your dog's name?"

"It's Shelley."

"Is this your boyfriend's dog?"

"Pop, it's Shelley, you remember hanging out with him on the couch."

It was only months ago.

My dad instantly erupts in tears, emotion sweeps over his face and he breaks down from the absence of memory.

"Carol, I don't remember nothing."

"You lost a lot of memory on the drugs didn't you, Pop? Sometime when you're ready, I'll show you the pictures I took in the hospital."

He sits down on the couch, "Bring 'em on, I'm ready."

"We can do it next week or next month sometime."

"Get 'em out now, I wanna see them."

There is only a handful but they are intense, with him hooked up to wires and blood-crusted hoses, looking like two Xs ought to be over his eyes.

I show him the first one. He keeps crying, but he soon starts to laugh.

"When little Paul said they come in to see me, he said he busted into tears. Now I see why."

We go through the other three and he returns to crying.

"I think it's funny, where I went. Look at that one, they got me cut open." And he peers at the slit they cut in his throat, to fit the breathing tube through.

"Well, your brother took me back to visit the nurses and while I was up there one of those dingers went off. That really took me someplace, musta remembered something from that."

The last picture is of me resting my face against my father's, eyes closed, holding the camera myself and capturing the soft moments I sang to him.

"Yeah, Dad, we were all scared."

"Well," he says, "least I know what I'm gonna look like dead."

"I remember when you went to the rehab wing and they had the back brace up around your chest."

"I remember it bumping up under my chin," he says. "It was like Keystone Cops in there, it was a nuthouse."

"Do you remember any of the hallucinations you had?" I ask.

"I remember we was in Vietnam then. Goddamned spiders were so big. Daddy-long-leg spiders. With these big long spindly legs and striped like bumblebees, yellow and black. My God those things scared me to death."

He recalls, "When I was in that goddamn place, the cleaning lady come in at four o'clock in the morning, *swish, swish*, she'd hit the bed every fucking time she rolled that mop over the floor.

"I said get the fuck out of here, will you? She said, *No, it's my job, gotta mop this floor.* Well get me a urinal then, I said. *Nope, it's not my job.* Well get the nurse for me. *Nope, it's not my job.* Well then, I said, I'm gonna just piss on the floor, then it'll be your job. She gave me the urinal."

We regard Dad as being on suicide watch. Danny and I fight over who should drive down to his house to check on him and keep him company. He sits in his rumbling diesel at the end of my sleepy cul-de-sac and taps eight pills from the bottle, throwing them back without even a swig of soda. He can't stop crying. A car deal Danny was wheeling didn't go down, Carol got a blood transfusion last week and is still recovering in a nursing home and the boy that used to fetch his phone out of the couch pillows has been shipped off to a foster home.

I offer my father the only thing I can to appease him; coupons for meat. Half-off dinners from restaurants that boast on their menu huge slabs of nothing but meat, glazed meat, roasted meat, barbecued meat, skewered meat, pulled meat.

"They got me going on methadone. I'm 56 years old and need a baby sitter."

I stand at my father's idling truck, my hand holding his through the window, harbouring a secret. I'm on the same panic medication as my father. *I'm 35 years old and I need a babysitter too.*

My father whizzes by ecstatic in his new red electric wheelchair, dubbed "The Jazzy" in a series of popular commercials.

"See my racing stickers, Sissy?" Flame decals lick down the sides giving the illusion of motion and a bumper sticker is plastered across the back; "Will race for food."

I snap a digital of me and Dad at the counter of Bob Evans.

"Look, Dad, look how great this is." I marvel at one of the only photographs of us together where there is not a twitch of danger seen in my face. "Wow, I even look pretty."

"Well, honey, you always been pretty."

I don't think my father has ever called me pretty.

"When you was a little baby, you used to hold those chickens we had out in Arizona."

My voice slips into masculine mode. "Yeah, I know." We did have chickens. Beautiful puffs of yellow fluff that we hatched from eggs in an incubator in the spare bedroom in Phoenix. I loved those chickens and held them so soft in my hand. When they were old enough, my father chased them through the backyard with an army buddy, lopping off their heads and tossing their

269

bodies into a cardboard refrigerator box. I watched him from the window over the dryer, watched how he laughed as a headless rooster ran terrified through the yard before keeling over dead. He only remembers me holding the baby chicks, I only remember him holding the neck of the rooster in his fist. It's the crossroad of memory where we will always part.

The waitress returns, her eyes light up. "Now I remember you, oh, yeah, I remember you now; it takes me awhile to remember faces."

"It's been a long time, baby," he tells her. "And I lost a 100 pounds since you saw me last."

He's lost about 50.

"We're gonna take you with us, give you a job down at my place," Dad flirts.

"I might come on down." She winks back.

I shoot her a look, *Don't encourage The King*.

Dad slinks out of his swivel barstool, the Bob Evans girl drives his Jazzy right up to his seat. This is the service you get when you live in Ohio.

Nothing wears me out like a small town Wal-Mart on a Sunday. It's like going to Disneyland in the school holidays. We drive across the road from Bob Evans and as I accompany my father in his quest to buy healthier groceries, Dad unloads the Jazzy off the special welded contraption he's rigged on the back of his truck. The ramps aren't quite lined up and one wheel dumps half the wheelchair in the parking lot with the other wheels cock-eyed on the platform. He wrestles with it and pulls it off the truck with a thump. In a flash, my father slips in the seat and he's off, dashing across the parking lot. I jog behind and hop on the two pegs that jut out the back, which are not intended for passenger use as a manufacturer's tag on the back warns me. But I'm riding it like a cart, my father amping up speed to crash through the automatic doors. Dan Andrety at the wheel, his *will race for food* bumper sticker caked with the dirt of a hundred other adventures like this. In my peripheral vision I catch an elderly woman just inside, toddling an empty cart into the store through the automatic doors, the same ones my father races towards.

"Dad, Dad, Dad, Dad, got a blue hair at two o'clock," and he side steers to the left just in time to miss her.

He crashes through the automatic doors himself and careens into produce, zipping in between people, throwing bags of carrots and stalks of broccoli over his shoulder. I grab a cart and race after, running behind his wheelchair; diving the cart under falling vegetables like a misguided game on *The Price Is Right*.

At the end of the aisle, he makes a sharp right and I say in my best radio voice, *You will now steer clear of the freshly baked cookies*. He slows to peer into sugary cases, I switch to my Asian favourite: *Hey, man-fat, you no need no cookie*s.

He jets off to the doughnuts.

I pretend to be a policewoman, talking into her loudspeaker. *Move away from the doughnuts. You will now move away from the doughnuts.*

We make it to the sausage section. "Get me one of them packs of maple-flavoured links, will ya, Sissy?"

"Pop, look at this one right here, same thing, but look, no corn syrup or honey and less grams of sugar."

"Bitch." he agrees and scoots off.

He stops at the tank of lobsters and waves, "Look Sissy, he waved back to me."

And it's all good fun, him talking like Cookie Monster, *me want cookie, me want cooookies* when we roll past the cookie dough section. But the bubble of Dad's good cheer is always subject to puncture.

We roll up to the dairy section as an older man stocks the shelves with yogurt. My father wants to stay close to the produce and does not want to move for the worker. He stops his Jazzy to pressure the man to move, but the guy, lost in the monotony of shelf stocking, moves back in with another box of yogurt.

My father inches to being two feet away from him. "How long do you think it's gonna take before this stupid son-of-a-bitch realizes he's in my way?" He turns to me. "Where'd he'd get his intelligence, grade school? Yeah, must have dropped him and dented his head when he was a baby."

And my father dissolves into retard talk, pressing further toward the man, provoking him. The elderly stock man obviously can't hear. Dad rolls back in disgust and zooms off and I follow, grabbing a yogurt from the shelf, even though my father never eats it.

It's another chance to slam dunk a human oversight and make the person feel like a moron, shoring up his own delusion that he's smart and savvy in the world.

And the lens only gets darker. As black people pour from the aisles my father digresses into how lucky we are.

"Come 'ere, I can't say this out loud." He pulls me close to his face. "We're lucky to have gotten in here today; they weren't checkin' ID for IQ levels. We're too high, they wouldna let us in."

A black woman barrels past him getting a box of cereal off the shelf; my father stops in front of her boyfriend.

"She ever stop for you?" He's masking it light, and the guy catches his drift, shakes his head.

"No man, usually I just follow her."

"I's just wondering if she ever stopped for you, 'cause she sure as hell wasn't gonna stop for me." And he cackles a disarming laugh, the insult so seamless her own man is none the wiser.

When I tell Dad I'm writing a book about our life together, he's overjoyed. He scribbles on a scrap of paper, *I, Dan Gregory, of sound mind and body – ha, ha, give permission for Julie to write about me*. I tell him I'd like to fly to Mom's and see if she has any pictures of us but that airline ticket prices are outrageous.

"It's called bereavement, Julie. All you gotta do is look up the obituary section of the newspaper you want to go to and call up the airline, tell 'em you're a cousin of the deceased and get a ticket for 89 dollars."

"Oh, Dad."

"You think Jews don't do that? Jews and Niggers? Hell, every nigger knows every other nigger in the world, didn't you see 'em at Wal-Mart Sunday, they was all talking each other on their cell phones."

"Dad, come on. You know I don't like it when you talk like that."

"I'm not a racist," Dad snorts. "Some of my best friends is niggers."

I am not writing a book, I'm living a book. I merely write myself into sanity, give my porous boundaries hard-edged lines, squeeze my ether self into the frame and shape of a girl contained; a girl who isn't leaking, leaking her very essence out of every pore. I wear my heart on my sleeve and it's bleeding. Makes for a real fucking mess.

Chapter Fourteen

*I*t is winter now and the ice encases the barren tree limbs until they are heavy and all shining crystal, glinting off sparks of shimmering light from the winter sun.

Danny and Dad pick me up for Christmas. It's his first big holiday out of the hospital; it would be sacrilege to avoid it. Our plan for the day is to see Carol, who is now in a different hospital, after getting another amputation of part of her foot.

My brother steps from the driver's side to greet me at the car. Having rushed out his door that morning, he stuffed a piece of fruit in his pocket. It's Christmas Day and per usual, we don't have any idea when or if we'll find something to eat.

"Now, is that a banana in your pocket or are you just happy to see me?" my father hoots.

In the back seat, I hum the theme from Johnny Carson, "Da nat da da da, dadadada." The Gregory Family Comedy Hour. The fun never stops.

I tell Danny that Dad was brave enough to look at the photos I took of him in the hospital.

"Well," Dad says, "that's what I'm gonna look like when I'm dead. But you know what Sissy, you won't have to bury me, I ain't never gonna touch the ground."

"'Cause you're getting cremated, right?" I say.

"Well, they're gonna have some fun with me first. I've donated my body to science. They'll give it to the kiddies at school. They take my body, play with it till they puke, then give Danny a dollar and give him back my body."

"They only give you a dollar for your body?" I ask.

"No, they give it to my next of kin, my son. What the fuck am I going to do with a dollar?" he roars. "God don't have a store. And if he did, he'd give you everything in it. You wouldn't need no dollar."

"God's dollar-rama," my brother quips. "Everything under a dollar."

I sit in the back seat, wondering why I'm not considered next of kin.

* * *

276

Halfway to the hospital, Dad has to pee. Still with a cracked pelvis and a walker to get around, when he has to go, he has to go. Danny pulls into a crowded gas station and we both help him out of the car. He scoots on his walker off into the store while Danny follows behind, trying to get people out of the way.

Back in the car, my father is incensed. He didn't make it in time.

"Goddamn fucking hillbilly, too busy waiting in line for cigarette lighters to get out of my way. I shoulda fucking peed on him."

Once at the hospital, the air is deathly quiet as I rummage through the car for an earpiece for Dad.

"Hurry up, Sis, I'm freezing," Danny complains.

"Back off, I'm looking for a crusty hearing aid back here."

In the quiet of the hospital corridor, I hear what sounds like a dog snoring.

"Dad, what's that wheezing sound?"

"It's my trach, see." He stretches his neck up to me; the wound looks like a sinkhole into his Adam's apple. "It's like a nose. It stinks. It gets boogers."

"You need a dickey, Dad."

We walk into the empty hospital cafeteria.

"Lunch is on me. It's not often I get to take my kids out to eat."

"Dad," Danny points to the obvious sign in front of us that says anyone here on Christmas doesn't have to pay, "It's free."

Carol lay beached in her hospital bed, reading a book, the result of her latest diabetes-caused amputation wrapped in white bandages, propped at an angle.

Dad wheels in the room. "Merry Christmas."

We stand around the bed.

"Damn, I forgot the eye patch and the parrot," Dad shoots.

"Eye patch?" I say.

"A parrot?" Danny asks.

"Yeah, all Carol needs is an eye patch and a parrot to go with her peg-leg and she can be a pirate!"

I cannot believe my father's uncouthness.

"That's okay, Julie," Carol laughs, "I'm used to it!"

I don't know what's worse; what he said or that she's used to it.

"Hey," Dad gets excited, "Can I use your library book to prop your leg up for the X-ray?"

"No! You can't use my library book," Carol shouts.

"I promise, it won't get too gooky."

"Can you imagine, someone at the library getting it?"

My brother and I exchange tired looks. It's like listening to two nine-year-olds banter back and forth.

Dad picks a piece of scab from his arm off with his teeth. He looks at the plastic bags Carol's gifts are in, that sit on her lap in the hospital bed.

"What you got in the bag, bitch?" he says.

"Dad!" I cry.

"She knows I'm joking."

Carol pulls out a colourful pillow, to add a spark of colour to her hospital room.

"I can't find the goddamn directions on the bag," my father says.

"I bet Hamburglar did it, stole the directions," Carol says.

Dad retells the story from the quickie mart. "So there were two lovebirds sitting in Circle K, looking at the lighters. I knew they weren't going to fucking get out of my way."

I walk into the hallway, happy to have a mission to get me away from the same story. When I return, I thrust my find at Dad, "Merry Christmas!"

"A urinal?" he squeals. "For me? Thanks Sissy, now I can piss in confidence knowing it won't run down my leg. Is this used?"

"Yeah, I took it off an old man's bedside. Of course it isn't used! I asked a nurse for it."

"Oh, goody, I can fill it up with Diet Coke and put a straw in it."

* * *

I excuse myself and go into the hallway. There aren't any chairs so I sit in a stray wheelchair.

My father rolls out of Carol's room. I feel touched he came to find me.

"Dad, what are you doing out in the hall?" I say, hoping he's come to have a quiet moment for all that's happened these last six months.

"I had to fart."

As the afternoon rolls in, we leave Carol and decide to have Christmas dinner at the local Chinese all-you-can-eat buffet. The lot is packed with cars and a solid sheet of ice covers the parking lot. With Dad in a walker, Danny pulls up next to the curb and parks in front of the large plate-glass window that is the front of the restaurant, close to the sidewalk. People sit at their tables with plates loaded with red barbecue spare ribs, egg rolls, chow mein noodles and slices of pizza. We help my father out of the car and my brother runs ahead to hold the door open, while I lock the car. Dad shuffles on the walkway in front of the plate-glass window and shouts, "Sissy, get me that urinal, I'm about to piss down my leg!"

I rush to him with the urinal and Danny, horrified, leans against the door, trapping a family inside from exiting. And right there, in front of the big plate-glass window and everybody chowing down, my father leans forward and relieves himself in the plastic tub. Danny races over to grab Dad's pants before they fall and my father, ready to roll, thrusts the wet handle of a warm urinal at me to dump in the snow. Another memorable Gregory family Christmas; it doesn't get any better than this.

"Saw wa dee cup?" my father says to the hostess, relying on his old standby for anyone who looks even remotely Asian.

The crowded restaurant is cheery and warm and my brother requests we be seated as far from the front window as possible. We sit around a table too big for the three of us and I hear the haunting voices of the children's choir sing from *A Charlie Brown's Christmas*. It is the perfect soundtrack for a classic holiday depression.

I lean over and hiss at my brother, "You suck. Not only did I have to feel around for his crusty hearing aid in the back seat, I had to dump his urinal in the parking lot."

"At least you didn't have to hold it," my brother says from behind a menu. "And I'm not talking about the urinal, Sis."

Spending the day with Dad can be exhausting; demanding stories, bottomless expectations, endless plans that go nowhere. And my brother, who once

281

used to be so easy going and enjoyable to be around, has become a tension-inducing control freak.

My brother argues he isn't uptight; he just likes a spotless car and a kitchen floor clean enough to eat off of.

My father says, "He just doesn't like Floyd licking off his plate while he's trying to eat. That's anal retentive for you." Dad lets out a wet belch.

Dad leans over my brother and wails on the horn, "Get the fuck out of the way, you moron."

I'm so tired from this Christmas. The grizzly bear that was once my father is just a crusty old circus tiger. But still; he soaks up everything, gives back not a drop.

When we get to my father's house, my brother gives Dad an early gift to open in the front seat.

"Oh, what is it, hard candy? Remember when I used to make us rock candy at the trailer? I'd take it in to work at the base and you couldn't keep that candy in the jar."

"Yeah, I know Dad, that's why I made it for you. It's homemade rock candy," my brother beams. His nostalgia for our father has driven him to spend hours in a barely used kitchen to try his hand making the stuff.

Dad turns over the tin and reads, "One dollar. Wal-Mart. Made in Taiwan."

My brother fumes, "It's homemade rock candy, Dad. I just put it in the decorative jar I got there."

"Oh, I see." My father seems dubious.

Danny gets out of the car to try to stuff the Christmas boxes in the trunk. Most of them are for Dad, presents bought to celebrate this holiday we thought we might not have again with him. Dad's walker sits leaned against the car, with all the other presents Danny has been hiding in the garage scattered around.

In the backseat, I secretly languish in full laziness as the girl. No longer willing to let myself get stuck out on the highway for the greater good of the family.

We can hear my brother cursing from outside the car. He is so tightly strung, I expect him to hurl something past the window. Two dogs walk up and bark at Danny. They take turns lifting their leg on one of the hand-polished spit-shined hubcaps of my brother's new car. He looks ridiculous kicking out at them, while balancing a huge box in his arms. I cannot contain my laughter, it's the pressure-release valve on the day.

"Jake and the fat lady," my dad says, looking at the dogs outside the car.

"Did I ever tell you about Frick and Frack? They was the raccoons that stole the Christmas bulbs in my garage." My father christens everything in the neighbourhood with the names he sees fit; old possums, other people's pets, their kids.

On the drive to Danny's house, Dad resumes talk about death.

"That's where I'll be, sitting in a jar of formaldehyde. Didn't you know where I'm going? I've donated my body to science, so after they've cut out my organs, they can send me to the incinerator. Then they'll scatter my ashes."

"No," Danny says, "We're going to put you in that '68," Dad's original GTO.

"In the trunk?"

"No, Dad, we don't put dead people in the trunk anymore. We'll just carry you around in the glove box, next to your gun."

Chapter Fifteen

I cannot condemn him for not being a good
father, for not protecting me. I can only glean
from the years the most simplistic of memories,
suspended out of context so that they may shine as
brightly as they possibly can. I can remember his hug
and good cheer at Danny's graduation, while ignoring
his same raucous laugh when one of his friends said,
Hey, you dropped your pocketbook, baiting me to bend
over in front of him and look for it. I can remember
my father for a spur-of-the-moment selfless act such
as when he drove his car trailer up to my house in a
blizzard to haul my broken truck away. And at the
same time I must selectively forget that while I struggled with the ramps to winch the truck on the trailer,

my creepy neighbour came out to talk to my father and told him I had a nice ass – and my dad just sat in the truck and didn't defend my honour.

Each memory I select has to be hosed off from a lesser or equal memory of the pain of something bad tacked to the good. I can remember how fun it was when he and Danny picked me up in Columbus on a Christmas so long ago, how I sat on my brother's lap and messed with his hair and we were just kids again. But on the way home, it was me who was asked to hitchhike for gas for the car. I became my own salvager from the wreckage of memories, much the way my father salvaged usable parts from totalled cars. Look hard enough and you can find something worth keeping, he would say. Probably the best advice he ever gave me.

Today, my father cries freely. He says, "I should'a known Sissy, I should have done something to protect you. I should have helped you kids. I should have told her to stop. I should have seen what she was doing. I could have done better."

I hold my father's hand in the restaurant, his unfinished plate of ribs drawing fruit flies. He slumps in his Jazzy and feels the full force of his words. He is speaking the truth and we both know it.

I do not tell him it's okay.

I do not tell him he was a good dad.

I do not tell him it wasn't his fault.

I let him feel it, knowing that he is only able to do so because of my strength.

He says, "It's not over yet Sissy, we'll have more good times, right?" Tears brim shiny in his eyes, those starving puppy eyes from day-care pictures at the base. And here come mine; I always hated those fucking pictures.

"We can go to the GTO Nationals together. You can drive one of our GTOs down there to the show. We can be a family again."

Empty promises, hollow words. My father desperately wants the family he has never had, not in his childhood, not with his own family and he has no idea how to get it.

None of us do.

I am expecting my first child. As I lie on my side in our bed, heaving sick, my partner hides in the woods and watches the house. He crashes through the bedroom door with a flashlight and sweeps it under the bed, me curled in it, looking for the man I am hiding under the frame. He bounds into the attic, taking the steps two at a time and shimmies up through the crawl space to stand in the rafters and turn over blown-in insulation. He is searching, racing back down the steps into the spare room to pull the bed from the wall and dig every last storage box from underneath to double check for the man he is sure I'm betraying him with. I stand in the doorway behind him, crying; one hand on belly, knowing my partner will not make it back to me, hoping he will make it back for our child.

At night as I sleep, he roots through old purses for scrap paper and empty chequebooks with random numbers scribbled on the back. He hunkers under the window and uses my phone to call them. If anyone answers at four in the morning, he asks them if I am there – even as I lie sleeping in our bed upstairs. People warn me that they think an ex-boyfriend is stalking me, calling their home in the middle of the night, looking for me. How can I tell them it's not an ex, but the man I love and that I carry his child.

My partner is beautiful, innocent, vulnerable. He has a snaggletooth. I would hold him till his deathbed. But he has been diagnosed with bi-polar and it is now, in the trigger of our pregnancy, that he is convinced I sneak men into the house to have sex with them – unlike my father who thought I snuck out.

Each day I would tidy up his house of thoughts, assuring him of our bond and reminding him of our prayers for a baby and each night he would run rampant through his thoughts and tip over the furniture. I wasn't just dealing with the loss of my love, but tacked to the underside, the tender wound of my father, the first man I loved so much I could never blame him for hurting me. I don't know why I couldn't see earlier. But it's too late now. My baby has come back to me. I will not make the same mistake twice.

I could not know how deep the wound of my father ran, mixed with love and blood. Or how my partner's tears were the perfect echo of my father's, and as much as he wore me down in panic, I was bound to him in love.

I felt omnipotent – as with my father – as the only one who understood him. And as in childhood, I locked myself in a room with his paranoia and tried to prove my innocence.

I tell myself I could not have known. But I should have. It was only through the alchemy of loving a man like my dad that I could claim the girl I once was. I have finally collected all the pieces of my childhood. Now I can hold them.

During the sweltering summer of my pregnancy, I call Dad for a favour. My car, sixteen years old, has once again broken down, leaving me stranded. Despite having an abundance of classic cars, I am brought the most decaying, grotesque 1989 sedan, with the driver's window broken, a wet cloth seat reeking of cat piss from the neighbourhood strays marking it, and the passenger side piled with empty bags of fast-food wrappings. It is the car the shop hands have been given to use. I clean out the cartons, stick a plastic rubbish bag on the seat and drive it for a few days, unable to figure out where the terrible stench is coming from. Only upon tearing up the floor mats do I see; fat maggots have burrowed into the moist carpet, rich with the juice of fast-food burgers and chicken fingers turned liquid in the August heat, having drawn flies in through the broken window. Five months pregnant and I am down on my knees, rolling them out of the carpet one by one. This is my family.

At her first rustle, I scoop up my baby at 5 am, sleep-lift her to my breast, her arms flop straight out to her sides. My two-week-old infant is a piranha who roots voraciously at my breast, clamping down with no less than a vice grip that makes me wince.

In the pale light of pre-dawn, I wonder if my own mother nursed me. I wonder if I was ever held like this, at 5 am in the most inconvenient moment for my father, his mouth wide open as he slept, catching flies. I cradle my daughter's skull gently in my hand; she sleeps so peaceably in the safety of my nest. I wonder if my father ever held my own fragile head in his hands. Or was it only me who held his in mine?

In the middle of the night, the cat walks over the baby, a fisted hand goes flailing over her head. I mark my pain from the C-section at her birth, the skin on my belly sears as if someone has been leisurely fanning a blowtorch over it. The baby has kicked me in the stomach now so many times the pain merely layers itself upon layers of previous pain.

I hear my baby girl's ghost cries in my ear, the way Mom heard rings of a ghost phone in hers. If anyone touches my daughter, I would shatter their every finger joint with a hammer. If anyone hurt my daughter, I would run them down with a car, over and over until tyre treads raised like baking bread on braised purple skin. The protection instinct, it's in me. And I have no idea where I got it.

In the first summer of my child's life, I wake in the middle of the night, pining for the man I still love, her father. The man who stole my clothes for DNA tests. The man who believed I snuck men in the house, to have them in our bed as he lay sleeping beside me. Everything sacred – my body, my pregnancy, my commitment, my love – made a mockery of. And still, I love him. But his sickness grew over his mind until he could not be with the infant or woman who so desperately needed him. And true to the curse that plagues me, I rinse the hurt and insanity from fleeting moments of happiness and hold them tight to my heart.

I feel so desperate for the embrace of an extended family that I offer my phone number on a scrap of paper to any grandmother in public that coos at my baby. I ask them to call me if they'd like to have lunch with us. They look at me blankly and I feel the sting of their judgement, my invitation sounding clunky and stupid as I play it over in my head. Despite being in the best restaurant and looking beautiful, I still feel like trailer trash when I hear myself explain that my child doesn't really have grandparents – not any that are coming to see her. The cost of bad blood is something I'll be paying off forever. It's a high-interest loan I'll never climb out from under.

Alone at night, with my baby tucked into the crook of my arm like a small downy bird, I will be her all; mother, father, family. My hips hurt, my back hurts, my heart aches with unsurpassable grief, for waiting so long and still ending up alone. I call my brother, desperate in my plea for him to see us and be just one man in the baby's life who will not leave her. But his call never comes. Each day I rearrange the thoughts in my head like furniture in my house, keeping order and cleaning the dirt, telling myself that it's going to be okay.

Each night I wake up in the middle of it, the furniture ransacked. Why couldn't he love me, why couldn't he protect me?

I had his child, I ask for one.

I was his child, I ask for the other.

Interchangeable, what I pine for in my partner is ultimately born of what I pined for in my father. And the answer's the same, because he couldn't.

I wasn't the only one who lost. Dad did too. He didn't just lose me as a child; he lost me as a daughter. The denial that he was ever paranoid, and the rampant control as he allows only those around him that pretend he's okay and bastardizes anyone who doesn't, makes it impossible for me to have anything but the most base of interactions with him. It is not what I want but it is all that is possible. My love for my father remains solid, but I know there is no use talking; he won't remember what he can't hear in the first place.

Living back in Ohio has all but engulfed me. No one understands why I reside in a part of the country where you can go through a Dairy Queen drive-thru and they pass you a pencil to sign your credit card receipt. Where people pump gas in overalls and you can still see a horse and buggy tied to a lamppost in the middle of a shopping centre parking lot; the Amish alive and well, living quietly among us. In a place where people still name their children Twain and Curtis, Dreama and Twila, and a giant American flag can endlessly ripple in slow motion atop a billowing smoke stack, spewing grey fumes across a country sky.

A once sharp juxtaposition of moving back to Ohio from London has been filed down smooth like long horse teeth. No edges remain. That I can roll maggots up out of a floor mat carpet burrow and see it as an extension of my family, their version of an olive branch extended to me when they give me such a putrid, decaying car after mine breaks down tells me that the growth that flung me out of here seven years ago has been grown over by a native vine; something beautiful but prolific, like honeysuckle – a choking nuisance if not cut back.

But there are beautiful parts to being here, driving the back-country roads. Fields of willowy golden rod, the setting sun shining through like stained glass. Ancient wooden barns faded red, as towering spikes of black-eyed Susans thrust up the sides, desperate to reach the sun.

And now I know myself: I fall in love through the written word. I'm a sucker for a beautiful face; emotional heavyweight champion of the world. I've lost everything I ever loved, then gained everything worth loving. I jazzercise to Ted Nugent's "Stranglehold", and am monogamous to stupefying bloody fault. I love the art of the long kiss. I move like an eel. I am rough-hewn beauty, my face rote with the hard line of trouble. And as for red high heels, I have several pairs.

Visiting a classic car show in the parking lot of the Chillicothe Veteran's hospital, I watch my father from a distance, yucking it up with my brother as they show one of their classic cars. My father among men, I will always be separate from him. My brother's shoulder blades wide and tawny beneath his thin designer T-shirt. They must have built an empire worth a million bucks; a sea of broken-down cars, stacks of classic chassis, rare and exotic rims. Back at their garage, a rusted hearse sits among a casket of weeds. The red fire hydrant in front of my father's garage is faded pink. It might not add up to the cash of a million but it is priceless to them.

I've watched my father and brother do so much in their crippled yet full life together, each of their inside legs bound to each other as they hobble into the future. But I stand alone. I tried to be like Dad, walking across gravel lugging his car parts. I tried to make him feel secure, scrubbing my beauty to both deflect his para-noia and help me feel safe with him. But I don't want to live bending at every seam like a reed. I want to stand in the middle of this road and strip down. I will chip away the shellac like so many pearly teenage fingernails, until I am all girl, flesh and bone; free from being a man to protect myself from men. In red high heels, head held high, not feeling like a slut, or a baby maker or a crack whore, just because my father thinks it's so. I will live for me now. My days of distorting myself to counter his distortion are over.

The first year of the baby's life I weather almost entirely alone. And by the second, I still am on my own. But something amazing has happened. I no longer try to tuck myself under the broken wing of a man. In the wake of becoming a mother, the past went down in flames. I had to burn him out. The man I searched for to love me, the man like my father, is no longer my compass. Never before could I even walk from an abuser, now my finely honed radar moves me on without apology. With child, what I might not have seen for myself, I see clearly now for both of us. Two years on my own calibrated me back to the love and instinct every child is born with. Some of us lose it along the way. Like a bowl of light piled with rocks until pitch black, I only had to take out each stone to get back my shine.

Almost through my thirties, I still find the beautiful girl inside; the one who defies age, who loves to dance to Eighties music, sing out loud in the grocery store, watch cartoons on the floor with my child. I have a working car now, a luxury I never would allow myself in the past; breaking the bind that tied me to my father, keeping myself destitute and broken down on the highway to see if he would rescue me. I can now rescue myself. And better yet, a woman resurrected from the ashes doesn't need much rescuing. I have a pink Italian villa, a kind of Liberace starter house, something outrageous and funky the performer might have lived in before he made it big. Outdated with sea-foam green carpet and peach wallpaper border from the 80s, it still has the good bones and sweeping high ceilings he would love. And most importantly, it is everything opposite of the trailer aesthetic I grew up with.

My child and I watch a summer storm blow in from the fields, the dark clouds roiling over light sky. The wind whips the screen, the sound deafening like tyres squealing on a truck, a ladybird holds on for her life as the screen flaps. We are alone in the eye of the storm and even in the immediate fright of it, I know it's going to be okay. A memory rises in me and on scrap paper I capture the essence of it in words. When I read it again, it evokes the original feeling of my experience. And then I see. I'm playing memory with my own life, turning over the cards inside and remembering where the match is. Everywhere I go, I play this game of memory. I see a flyer for a missing girl. It's a photo of her smiling face, tilted in just such a way. She is 17, last seen climbing into the back seat of a car with an unknown man. I want to pair the parents of missing daughters with the daughters born to missing parents.

Flyers for lost animals, flyers for lost girls, all things lost, I want to walk the world, connecting the dots, putting things back in their rightful place.

Swirls of blackbirds flush from the sky, spinning ribbons back and forth against the flat dusk of winter. I sit at a city traffic light to watch them and dissolve into tears. The beauty of this unpredictable, crazy life; it's the only thing that moves me. Grace, my ability to mother a child, the capacity to love, born of nature not nurture. I am my own keeper; this is my job now, to find profound beauty and break the silence of the past.

In this fleeting moment, I feel alive, free again, small, beautiful.